Penguin Education

Papers in Education

**Simulation in the Classroom**
John L. Taylor and Rex Walford

'Seven — you take your cavalry back to the hill, I capture all your artillery and advance to the edge of the moat.'

# Simulation in the Classroom

(An introduction to role-play, games and simulation in education with six established games described in detail and a directory of published material)

John L. Taylor and Rex Walford

Penguin Education

Penguin Education
A Division of Penguin Books Ltd,
Harmondsworth, Middlesex, England
Penguin Books Inc, 7110 Ambassador Road,
Baltimore, Md 21207, USA
Penguin Books Australia Ltd,
Ringwood, Victoria, Australia
Penguin Books Canada Ltd,
41 Steelcase Road West,
Markham, Ontario, Canada

First published 1972
Reprinted 1974
Copyright © John L. Taylor, Rex Walford, 1972

Made and printed in Great Britain by
C. Nicholls & Company Ltd
Set in Monotype Times New Roman

There is no point in work
Unless it absorbs you,
Like an absorbing game.
If it doesn't absorb you,
If it's never any fun,
Don't do it.

D. H. Lawrence

# Contents

## Part Three
## Sources of Material for the Classroom  145

# Preface

This text was commissioned by Penguin Education to introduce classroom simulations and games to a more general audience. In essence, it is intended to provide a brief guide and operational introduction to the state of this fast-developing art.

We have divided the book into three main Parts. The first considers the evolution and relevance of simulation and related techniques; the second provides representative samples of work which have already been successfully employed in the classroom; and the third Part identifies readily available material of particular value to readers about to extend their working knowledge and skills in this area.

At best, this text will be used as a basic primer, operational handbook and reference work. If it serves as a stimulus to greater experimentation and more discriminating discussion about simulation, we shall be well satisfied.

Following on from this point, it is clear that simulation development, like other educational innovations, relies on the continual patience of enthusiastic practitioners and their willingness to share insights and ideas with others; in this sphere, we wish to thank all those with whom we have had contact, and especially, the designers of the six simulations in Part Two who readily agreed to place their material at the disposal of a wider audience.

Similar expressions of gratitude, for backing and support, are owed to many colleagues, students and agencies, too many to be identified individually. However, particular thanks must be extended to all those at the University of Sheffield, Maria Grey College, Twickenham, the Royal Institute of British Architects, and the Nuffield Foundation, who have given valuable assistance throughout our efforts to widen our simulation experience.

Finally, it must be acknowledged that simulation – and writing about simulation – can be a time-consuming business. In this respect, we owe much to the cheerful forbearance and the willing assistance of our wives.

# Part One
# An Introduction to Instructional Simulation Techniques

# Chapter 1
# What is Simulation?

One afternoon in 1970, a group of millionaires sat down around a table at the London Hilton Hotel. They included such tycoons as Oliver Jessel, Jim Slater and Sir Jack Cohen (the owner of the Tesco supermarket chain); other members of the gathering included a couple of top-ranking financial journalists and the actor and man-about-town, Robert Morley. Under the glare of television lights, the group spent a couple of hours exchanging properties and money. At the end of the session, Sir Jack Cohen was generally acknowledged to have bankrupted the others, and as they rose from the table there were gentlemanly smiles and handshakes all round.

The situation for Sir Jack's rivals was not quite as devastating as might be imagined, however; they were bankrupt only in terms of the game of Monopoly. The session had been a BBC producer's bright idea for TV, to see how real-life tycoons performed in one of the most famous simulation games yet devised. There are plenty of households where the feeling of being a property tycoon has been experienced – at least in a partial way – through the playing of this well-known home entertainment. Monopoly is a simulation game since it seeks to represent a real-life situation with a simpler 'model' version of the situation, albeit something of a caricature.

If the term simulation seems unfamiliar in relation to this particular experience, there may well be other places where the reader will have noted its use as a description, even when its technical meaning has not been fully explicit.

The 'Link trainer' used to train RAF pilots in the Second World War was one of the earliest devices to be consciously described as a 'simulation'; it was a dummy cockpit set up in a hangar or an office-block with a canvas hood over it. Once inside, the learner pilot was alone with the controls – and what he did in the simulator was reflected on counters and dials outside it, watched by senior and more experienced performers. The 'Link trainer' allowed the pilot to experience a 'model' of the actual flying situation; it also allowed him to see what mistakes he might make, and to escape from them punishment-free. The simulator was giving experience and acting as an instrument of self-teaching.

More recently, the word 'simulation' has flashed up on TV screens up and down the nation with regularity, as science correspondents and astronomers have sought to explain the intricacies of the moon probes. Even though they are still denied complete television coverage of every lunar module's every move, simulation models have demonstrated what should, what might, what could happen. In the same way, the astronauts themselves have received all their training by the development of simulated situations, in something very akin to the Link trainer of the 1940s.

It is eight-thirty in the upstairs room of the Ordnance Arms, Southwark. Across a green-baize table-top a dozen careful pairs of hands move and remove groups of foot-soldiers, cavalry and artillery. From time to time a steel-tape is brought out to measure distances; then a dice is thrown. There is a little talk, a good deal of consulting of rule-books, and occasionally a suppressed smile as a particular dice-roll removes a commander from the field. On this occasion, the Battle of Barnet, 1471, does *not* see the White Rose in triumph; instead of Edward Plantagenet pressing forward northwards, his troops retire in some disorder to London. History has not repeated itself in this war game simulation, played with care for fidelity by the London Society of Ancients.

War gaming, unlike business gaming, is usually carried out with no ulterior motives. Military enthusiasts re-fight the battles of the past, invent battles of the future. There is no guarantee that battles will turn out to be exact replicas of events (though the Japanese are reputed to have lost the Battle of Midway precisely because a pre-game battle simulation was 'twisted' by a Japanese general who fudged an umpire's decision rather than admit that the plan was unsound tactically). Chess is believed to be the original 'war game' and despite its current high degree of symbolism, its antecedents are unmistakable.

In a theatre in a Midland town, nearly a thousand children sit enthralled. Aided by evocative music, sound effects and the consummate skill of actors who are improvising as the situation changes, the children are drawn into a 'journey to the centre of the earth'. It is not a pre-planned show; the children decide which route shall be followed, and what equipment shall be taken. 'From their seats, they climb ropes, dig for precious minerals, and plunge down narrow rock chimneys. The plot, like the programme of a many branched teaching machine goes where it is told; themes can be developed or omitted entirely'. The director of the show, interviewed by a journalist, repudiates what he is doing as 'children's theatre' – 'It's an imaginative experience in its own right, an extension of the games which children play in everyday life.'

The use of the 'game experience' is, as this director points out, no strange thing to children. From the days when they enter the woodshed and put on the costumes in the old drama box, or enter into the complex fantasy world of children's playground games, they adopt the idea quite naturally. And thus the imaginative 'simulation' of the journey to the centre of the earth can be understood with a minimum of difficulty. It does not have the structural complexity of the war-game rules, or even the 'seriousness' of the business game, but it represents a branch of the family of 'simulation ideas' nevertheless.

But all this, a patient reader may conclude, seems to have little to do with the title of this text. Games and simulations for property tycoons at play, for avid military enthusiasts, and even for school-children in their leisure time are some way from their use in a more general educational context.

The examples given above are certainly not obviously related to education itself; but they do represent something of the range and variety of simulation techniques. To present a more balanced view of simulation at work we need to consider one further example.

In a tenth-grade classroom in a Catholic High school in Minnesota, a nun is teaching a class of sixteen-year-old girls. At least, she is present *in* the classroom, but not actually controlling it at this moment. The class is split into groups of pupils, most of whom seem to be engaged in animated discussion.

As the teacher moves to overhear one group, she finds the Chairman of the discussion summing up.

'I'm sorry Frances, but I don't think that we can let this matter of cheap labour completely *dominate* our thinking; the company has clearly to take it into account, but only as far as a marginal factor. I tend to agree with Diane that market potential is far more important in relation to future growth.'

'O K President, I agree ' says another girl 'but don't you think that Denver is a suicidal choice in relation to our raw material supplies?'

The group react vigorously to this, and turn on the speaker with murmurs of dissent.

What is going on is an exercise from the American High School Geography Project, a curriculum project on which nine years' work and two and a half million dollars have been spent. This is a part of the unit on manufacturing, and it is a central activity to the unit. It is a simulation exercise called 'Locating the Metfab Company' and its aim is to teach about the factors that influence the location of industry.

Play is understood universally, by adults just as much as by children, to whom it is instinctive. Much play is simulation play, with participants acting out situations in which they assume the place of somebody else; and this extends from the make-believe of the Wendy-house to the carefully organized lawyers' mock-trial.

There seems every reason to believe that elements of simulation play can be transferred or adapted from their existing contexts and used consciously as an approach to learning. This is not to suggest that Monopoly boards should invade every classroom (though no doubt the game has its points to make); but rather that the style of activity which simulations and games represent should become an accepted mode of teaching.

What happens in any simulation (whether it is Monopoly, the Battle of Barnet, a journey to the centre of the earth, or the location of Metfab) is that:

1. Players take on roles which are representative of the real world, and then make decisions in response to their assessment of the setting in which they find themselves.

2. They experience simulated consequences which relate to their decisions and their general performance.

3. They 'monitor' the results of their actions, and are brought to reflect upon the relationship between their own decisions and the resultant consequences.

Whether the simulation has structure or not, interrelationships between a large number of factors can be displayed, visibly manipulated and adjusted. As the situation develops, so new strategies need to be formulated and adopted. (As every Monopoly player knows, the hazards on the board change from round to round; so that sometimes, late in the game, to 'Go to Jail' is a relief, rather than a disadvantage!)

We hope, in this book, to explore the educational implications of simulation for the classroom. We will be concerned to clarify the nature and the potential of gaming-simulation procedures, and to analyse their possible uses. But throughout the text it may be useful to remember that the techniques under discussion are recognizable outgrowths of familiar everyday games – such as chess, Monopoly, and 'let's pretend'.

# Chapter 2
# Historical Background

## Nature and origins

Simulation techniques are centuries old; it is only their importation into the classroom that is a recent phenomenon. A direct linear progression of events which precede current simulation activity is not easy to discern, but certain historical landmarks can be identified.

It may be most helpful to examine these in relation to the three major streams of simulation: role-play, gaming and machine or computer simulation.

### Role-play

Role-play relies on the spontaneous performance of participants, when they have been placed in an hypothetical situation. It is undoubtedly the simplest form of the three types of simulation considered here, since it usually has little formal structure. All that is required is for the participant to accept a new identity, step inside someone else's shoes, and act and react as appropriately as he is able. What may happen in role-play is anyone's guess; there are no formal restraints on a situation, even if the group involved may be aware of some general objectives. If an international conference is to be acted out, then delegates may feel constrained to argue furiously, walk out, say nothing, or (in imitative style) bang their shoes on the table. None of these things are prescribed, none prohibited.

In role-play the essential core of the activity is understanding the situation of another person. A pupil is hopefully placed in a position in which he is given the opportunity to 'feel' what is at stake (given basic information). Then follows the experience of relating the situation to the differing situation of others – the problem of interacting with others. Through such participation, it is hoped that pupils gain a greater understanding of other roles and relationships, as well as a better awareness of what they themselves are doing.

The origins and development of this technique appear to be the most obscure of the three major simulation streams, perhaps because of the very simplicity of role-play. It is quite likely that such activity, undignified by the thought that it was a 'technique', has had fairly widespread use.

Its extension into more sophisticated and more overt and conscious use seems to have developed in the 1930s. At that time a growing interest in small-group behaviour by psychologists, psychiatrists and sociologists led to the use of role-play as a vehicle for extending research into human behaviour in varied learning environments. It also led to the use of role-play as a form of therapy for mental sickness, e.g. Moreno's work with 'psycho-drama'. Josephine Klein's book *Working With Groups* (1964) was an influential text in carrying through the idea in the cause of better personal relationships, and was the forerunner of much modern work in this field.

From quite another direction came the development of drama as a liberating and self-educating activity for pupils in schools; something which was quite distinct and almost opposite to the 'appreciation of the theatre'. The fact that there was a 'school play' did not necessarily mean that drama was being used educationally in many institutions – quite the reverse, with un-willing introverts being urged to do their piece for the 'good of the school'. But also in the 1940s drama was appearing on regular timetables in some schools for the first time, and an increasing number of drama teachers came from training colleges to establish the subject in schools in its own right. They used drama lessons not only to 'read plays' but to develop a sense of character and experience in pupils; and though this had affective rather than cognitive intent in a majority of cases, the idea of role-play became a common one in free-form situations in drama or English lessons.

The 1950s and 1960s saw the growth of 'Theatre-in-Education' projects, sponsored by local repertory theatres, which visited schools and nurtured this growth, or sowed initial seed, as was appropriate. The tremendous success of most of these ventures has underlined the general value of drama in schools, quite apart from the particular aspect of it which is under consideration in this text. Brian Way's influential *Development through Drama* (1967) is a useful indication of this kind of activity; not least because it suggests the value of drama not only in specialist lessons, but as a teaching methodology in many other subject areas.

## Gaming (*gaming-simulation/operational gaming*)

This is a slightly more complex activity because it relies on more formalized procedures and a greater structure of relationships. Games customarily consist of groups of players (decision-makers) placed in a prescribed setting, with constraints in this setting represented by rule systems and methods of procedure.

The behaviour and the interaction of players in a game can possibly involve competition, cooperation, conflict or even collusion, but it is usually limited or partially prescribed. An initial situation is identified and some direction given about the way the simulation is expected to work. Some games nevertheless are still primarily concerned with the desire to 'understand the decision-making process', as in role-play; others, however, may be moving towards a prime desire to 'understand the model' or examine the process which the game itself represents.

Gaming simulation procedures have both a venerable and a clearly discernible pedigree relating primarily to war-games. For example, the Chinese war game of 'Wei-hai' (meaning encirclement) is estimated by Andrew Wilson (1968) to have originated about 3000 B.C. Today, its modern equivalent is generally regarded to be the Japanese game 'Go'. Chess is probably a derivative of one of these earlier forms of encirclement game. However, it was not until the turn of the eighteenth century, with the growing belief that war was rapidly becoming less of an art and more of a science, that gaming began to be viewed as an important approach to training. The ensuing military search for increasing efficiency led to greater and more widespread investment in the technique – a situation which has held good from the middle of the nineteenth century to the present day. The First World War, for instance, was preceded by elaborate and extensive war-game manoeuvres on both sides. In 1963 there were listed officially some two hundred operational war gaming models, excluding many used purely for very basic military training (Wilson, 1963). The same author went on to state his belief that this number was probably being doubled at about two-yearly intervals. Certainly, in terms of money and energy, the resources devoted to war gaming show little sign of being on the decrease; for example, the US Navy Electronic Warfare Simulation (NEWS) was estimated recently to have cost seven million dollars.

## Machine or computer simulation

This branch of simulation activity is rooted in mathematics. Probability theory, game theory and other associated mathematical techniques are utilized to build in chance and random elements to simulated activities, and these are usually processed by electronic calculator or computer.

Sometimes it is possible to use these as a teaching tool in quite simple ways (e.g. in the expression of the probabilities of a simulated game of darts, or of cards) and several schools have developed simple simulation of space technology on this basis. Most frequently, however, machine simulation is related to a higher level of complexity than the other two types, since the computer can handle excessive numbers of variables in a way that is impossible for the human brain.

The purpose of machine simulation is usually to find 'answers' rather than to understand processes, and with data, chance factors and ultimate factors programmed into a machine, human participation is limited to an initial development of the programme and a response to a final result. It is possible to use machine simulations with interest if repeated variations of a problem are being worked through, but the amount of participation in the simulation process is clearly limited.

Such simulation techniques have been applied not only to the prediction of such events as the election of the American president, but to the intriguing possibilities of 'Hall of Fame' boxing matches (Marciano v. Ali), horse-races (pre-runs of the Derby), and even cricket Tests, in which players from differing eras of the sport are represented (England v. Australia, January 1972). The computer is able to simulate the unpredictability of the sport, allied to the known skills of the performers, in at least a reasonable way.

More seriously, the computer has been used in simulation to speed the operational research process. As Pool (1964) has pointed out, electronic machines have provided an instantaneous way of handling numerous interacting propositions in a variety of manners. To explore an equivalent range of propositions using human agents alone would often be prohibitively cumbersome and time-consuming.

The 'mathematical simulation' represented in Part Two of this book (Urban Growth Model) does not presume computer access; if it did so, the most time-consuming part of the operation (choice of random-numbers and allocation of points) would become minimal. The simulation is useful, nevertheless, in demonstrating the basis of mathematical simulations of this kind.

As computer availability has increased, so the possibility of taking the 'busy work' out of calculations has been utilized. Some orthodox games and simulations suggest that computers may be useful in doing this; a good example is the successful game developed for schools by the Institute of Chartered Accountants (The National Management Game). This uses computer calculations to provide fast feedback to schools after they have taken their weekly decision concerning the hypothetical firm that they manage; as a result, complex variables can be handled easily and interest in the game maintained.

These three strands of development form the background to the contemporary scene in simulation. These developments have occurred mainly (though not exclusively) in the social sciences, gaining popularity through the innovation and experimental climate of education in the 1960s.

The distinction between these three types of simulation is not clear-cut and definitions in this field are still a matter of considerable dispute. There obviously can be considerable overlap between role-play, gaming and machine simulation; a simulation *game* can be constructed to contain role-play of an extensive kind (see The Conservation Game and Congress of Vienna in Part Two); it can also require the use of a calculator or computer to expedite its procedures.

In this context, finer distinctions seem relatively unimportant, however; suffice to say that we use the three broad classifications as a general ordering device in what follows.

**Recent developments**

*Business gaming*

Business games were a direct growth from war games, and owe much to initiatives begun in 1956 by the American Management Association. These moves culminated in the design of A M A's Top Management Simulation which received instantaneous recognition (Riccardi *et al*, 1957). Almost overnight, gaming became a popular training activity for universities in this field, as well as for industry and commerce.

The attractiveness of the technique, coupled with the buoyancy of modern business activity, has led to the design of over two hundred different business games in the last decade. Today's business games range from fairly simple decision-making exercises lasting little more than an hour, through to extremely elaborate simulations involving perhaps several days to complete a single round of decision-making. The B B C have screened two management education series, using simulation techniques to identify general business problems. British European Airways, for example, use a week-long British Training Airline game to train young executives and managers; institutions such as Ashridge Management College use simulation material as a general part of their courses.

The application of this technique to the classroom was begun in England by the Esso Students Business Game, which had its first trials in 1968. More recently, as noted above, the Institute of Chartered Accountants, in cooperation with International Computers Ltd and the *Financial Times*, launched an inter-school game designed to give fifth and sixth formers an experience of 'board-room type' decision-making. (Each game is played by three companies in competition with each other; they start with identical resources and make four to six moves. A game lasts about three weeks, with school decisions being communicated to a central computer centre; there are 'heats' and then 'finals'. In 1969–70, two hundred and forty-three schools in England and Wales took part.)

Other games have been developed for use within individual classes and schools and Chemical Manufacturing (see Part Two) may be seen as representative of these. The general aim of these games is to communicate management principles and business skills (but not necessarily ethics) in such diverse areas as marketing, production stock control, and labour relations. The resources invested in business games appear to be immense and may even rival the contemporary commitment to military gaming.

## Gaming in the social sciences

The development of war and business gaming influenced, in its turn, the evolution of ideas in the social sciences. Formalized 'think tanks' such as that initiated at the Research and Development Corporation of America (RAND), and associated advances in computer technology, operational research and systems thinking began to influence many scholars in their approach to social phenomena. A more rigorous application of scientific methods ensued, and discussion of social technology became commonplace (Helmer, 1965).

Early applications of this were in the field of political and 'crisis' gaming, notably by Guetzkow at Northwestern University (1959). His Inter-Nation Simulation was refined and developed as a tool in the teaching of international relations over a number of years, and more recently it has been turned into kit form and used in American, Canadian and English schools.

Miles Copeland (1969) has written about the real-life implications of this type of study, and revealed its influence in some aspects of American foreign policy making. In some respects, the technique was used unwisely as a predictive device. Copeland himself was notably concerned in one of the first televised simulations in Britain, a 'Horizon' BBC programme, based on a three-day simulation of the Arab-Israeli crisis held at St Anne's College, Oxford in 1969.

Urban development gaming has also expanded at a remarkable rate as planning has become more a total science and less exclusively concerned with the technological aspects of bricks and mortar. Hence planners have built upon the games developed by business analysts, economists, political scientists, organizational psychologists and sociologists to present a more balanced synoptic view of urban phenomena. In essence, their games are dynamic representations of selected aspects of the human settlement; they describe, simply, the milieu within which the planner works.

Urban-development gaming is not only a testimony to the diversity of interest focused on the technique in the social sciences; it is also a useful guide to the different functions served by gaming simulation in this area. Just as Nicholson (1970) distinguished a multiplicity of purposes for which simulation seems appropriate in the analysis of international systems, so the task can be done for urban gaming. There now exists an extensive range of simulations designed for education and training, hypothesis generation and testing, and charting the alternative possible course of dynamic situations over periods of time (Taylor, 1971).

*Simulation in schools*

Boocock and Schild (1968, pp. 15–18), in commenting on American experience of simulation games for the classroom, identify three distinct (if overlapping) phases of development:

*Phase 1: 'Acceptance on faith'*. They believe this phase to have lasted until 1962–3, and to have been the time when 'games' were being 'discovered' as a classroom technique. More time was spent on designing games rather than evaluating them, and there was a consequent rush of enthusiastic reports tempered by little hard evidence about the effect of games in the school situation.

*Phase 2: 'Post-honeymoon period'*. They see this as a period when various researchers attempted controlled experiments with games, producing either negative or inconclusive results. They quote Robinson's evaluation of the Northwestern University's Inter-Nation Simulation mentioned above, which provided inconclusive results in testing whether students who used the simulation had learnt more than those who did not. (At the same time Boocock and Schild point out some of the weaknesses of the evaluation study.) A paper by Cherryholmes (1966), synthesizing a number of other reports, concluded that games do motivate, but that there was not any evidence that they teach facts or problem-solving skills, or that they induce critical thinking any more than any other methods of learning.

*Phase 3: 'Realistic optimism'*. Boocock and Schild go on to suggest that (in the American situation at least) there are now more realistic approaches to simulation material as a wider variety of games is developed, as their appropriateness for differing situations is better understood, and as there is revision or clarification about what games can or cannot do in the classroom. Their book goes on to develop these hopes in a variety of chapters contributed by different authors.

It may be helpful here to also identify several innovative forces and projects which have been responsible for the development of simulation material in the classroom; though the general use and application of the ideas is now widespread, much of the original work stemmed from sources in North America.

*People*

Jerome Bruner has for some time been eminent in the attempts to satisfactorily describe the 'learning process' and a 'theory of instruction'. More recently, with support from the Ford Foundation, he has directed a Social Studies Curriculum Program, 'Man: A Course of Study'. Both in his general writings on education, and in his own curriculum schemes, Bruner has highlighted the academic utility of simulation ideas, and the benefits which they offer (1967):

The most persistent problem in social studies is to rescue the phenomena of social life from familiarity without at the same time making it all seem 'primitive' and bizarre. Four techniques are proving particularly useful in achieving this end. The first is contrast ... the second is the stimulation and use of informed guessing, hypothesis making, conjectural procedures. The third is participation – particularly by the use of games that incorporate the formal properties of the phenomena for which the game is an analogue. In this sense, a game is like a mathematical model – an artificial but often powerful representation of reality. The fourth is the ancient approach of stimulating self-consciousness ...
  Games go a long way toward getting children involved in understanding language, social organization, and the rest; they also introduce ... the idea of a theory of these phenomena. We do not know to what extent these games will be successful but we shall give them a careful try. They provide a superb means of getting children to participate actively in the process of learning – as players rather than spectators (pp. 92–3, 95).

A second influential figure in the development of simulation has been James Coleman, head of the Department of Social Relations at Johns Hopkins University. Coleman has been the stimulus for many of the ideas and much of the research on simulation, and Boocock and Schild acknowledge their own debt to him in the preface to their 1968 book. With the assistance of funds from the Carnegie Foundation, the Centre for the Study of Social Organization of Schools at Johns Hopkins has done much to identify problem areas in contemporary education and opportunities offered by simulation. Coleman and his Academic Gaming Associates have continued to emphasize the functional possibilities of games in schools as distinct from their cognitive and affective influences.

(Some) games pluck out of social life generally (including economic, political and business life) a circumscribed arena and attempt to reconstruct the principal rules by which behaviour in this arena is governed and the principal rewards it holds for its participants. Such a game, both in its construction and in its playing, then becomes of extreme interest to the student of social organization. For from it he may learn about those problems of social relations that are his central concern. The game may provide for him that degree of abstraction from life and simplification of life that allows him to understand better certain fundamentals of social organization . . .

But the question immediately arises, how possibly could a professional sociologist and a sixth or twelfth-grade child learn about social life from the same game? My answer is that it is precisely appropriate that this be so. For children have been too long taught things that are 'known' and have too seldom been allowed to discover for themselves the principles governing a situation.

(From the Preface to 'Simulation games in learning').

### Agencies

The art of designing games was seen, in the United States in the early 1960s, as something more than everyman's occupation. Consequently, as simulation activity proliferated there came into being agencies in which specific simulation expertise was concentrated.

Clark Abt, an early game developer, brought into being Abt Associates Inc. in 1965, a commercial organization which concentrates on building educational and training game systems.

Abt Associates were the designers of the Agile-Coin game which was commissioned by the Advanced Research Project Agency in 1964 in order to find out more about the problems of 'internal revolutionary conflict'. The difficulties which American troops were finding in fighting in Vietnam were the direct cause of this request. Besides an interest in this area, Abt Associates have been extensively involved in the development of classroom simulations at all levels. For example, Pollution and Neighborhood were both designed as community-oriented simulations at the request of the Public School System of Wellesley, Massachusetts. Similarly, the game of Manchester was designed by Abt under contract to an organization called Educational Services Incorporated.

Abt Associates have also been involved in the development of games for some of the recent American curriculum projects. Aspects of this work have been documented by Abt himself (1970) and by Alice Kaplan Gordon (1968) a former Abt worker who wrote eight monthly booklets for SRA as a contribution to teacher in-service programmes in the USA.

A second agency, now independent, is Project Simile which arose from work first funded by the Western Behavioural Science Institute at La Jolla, California. Project Simile was first coordinated by Hall Sprague and Garry Shirts, and more recently has been headed by Shirts alone. Its particular reputation has been concerned with the development of simulations in the humanities field, and it has focused on the way in which games arouse interest and change attitudes. Shirts himself expresses a healthy scepticism about some of the 'over-claim' made for simulation, but appears to have been successful in introducing simulation ideas to a wide school audience.

Project Simile's most famous simulation is the deceptively simple Starpower in which groups of participants are issued with sets of chips to 'trade'. The simulation has a potentially explosive conclusion, and is advertised as being one for 'adventurous and courageous teachers'. An envisaged ending to the game is that one or more of the participants will refuse to continue to play. It can lead, however, to valuable and stimulating consideration of the problems of 'under-development' or 'under-privilege'. What the simulation achieves is in giving the players the chance to experience (unconsciously) the feeling of what it is like to be poor.

Plans and Sitte are other well-used simulations from the Project, and are rivals, even in the open market, to games which are produced from commercial sources for entertainment purposes.

*Projects*

The American Government has funded curriculum reform projects with considerable generosity in the last decade, and, as a result, such projects have had time to consider and evaluate teaching methodologies in a comprehensive way. Several of these have considered and used simulations (and the work of Bruner's Social Studies Project has already been noted).

The American High School Geography Project ran for nine years from 1961, and was funded with a total of two-and-a-half million dollars. In the early part of its life it was concerned with an attempt to develop a definite course taught by means of TV video-tapes, but the Project changed course on the appointment of Nicholas Helburn to the Directorship in 1964, and from then on concentrated its resources on much more pupil-centred activities.

In the period when the first batch of the material was on trial in a large number of schools, both teachers and students were asked to rank the activities of the Project's course work in terms both of interest and 'sense of worth'. Out of a total of twenty-three activities, the three simulations came out in the following rank order:

Teachers – interest: 1st, 2nd, 5th
Teachers – sense of worth: 1st, 2nd, 5th
Students – interest: 1st, 2nd, 4th
Students – sense of worth: 1st, 2nd, 4th

As a result of this the Project increased the proportion of simulation material in their subsequent units, and it represented over half the activities in the later sections of their work.

Some of the Project's simulation activity was designed by outside agencies (e.g. Section was commissioned from Abt Associates), and other parts were developed by the authors of the course units themselves.

*Simulation in British schools*

Following a good deal of informal and even unconscious use of simulation techniques, general experimentation in Britain was given a conscious fillip by word of American initiatives. In the past five years, as far as anyone can tell, there has been much increased use of simulation, most notably in the fields of social studies, general studies, history and geography.

Without the financial backing that American projects have enjoyed, however, such experimentation has been fragmented and difficult to document. Many useful ideas have spread from one classroom to another only by word of mouth, or by accidental dissemination through mimeographed documents. No comparable institutions to the simulation agencies such as Abt or Project Simile exist, nor is there yet any journal to rival *Simulation and Games*. In 1969, the Society for Academic Gaming in Education and Training (SAGSET) was brought into being, following a conference at Berkshire College of Education; SAGSET now acts as a clearing-house for many pieces of simulation material and it is run as a voluntary and spare-time activity by its organizers. Its main activities are a summer conference, an advisory service and a newsletter.

Current curriculum projects do seem to be taking simulation techniques into their system, however. The Schools Council Humanities Project, based latterly at the University of East Anglia, has been seeking to develop a more open-ended approach to discussion situations in the humanities, and has included a simulation game, Crisis in Lagia (a thinly-veiled analogy of the Vietnam situation), in its materials. There has also been a good deal of role-play material included in the work developed by the Moral Education Curriculum Project at the University of Oxford's Institute of Education.

Tansey and Unwin (1969) have documented some of the early developments in England. Notable amongst this early work are the simulation ideas used with very young children by Smith and Cole (1967), later developed amidst other basic conceptual teaching material by Cole and Beynon (1969; 1970; 1971).

## Simulation in educational training

In commenting on the evolution of academic ideas and the related diffusion process in schools, it may be useful to comment on parallel developments directed towards teachers.

In America, the Jefferson Township School Simulation concentrated on a simulation of the behaviour of school principals (Hemphill *et al.*, 1962); it was an outgrowth from administrative training procedures more common in the business world. A series of in-basket exercises (matters arising from the hypothetical morning post) in addition to film and tape recordings of hypothetical situations and conversations, all require the participant to assume the role of principal and offer the opportunity of practising appropriate decision-making. Pre-service teacher training in the USA followed this lead with packaged simulated classrooms constructed by Cruickshank (1966), Kersh (1962) and Twelker (1967) among the first in the field.

P. J. Tansey and D. Unwin at Berkshire College of Education were among the first in Britain to develop a similar approach and jointly developed simple simulation exercises which replicated problems in the classroom for student teachers. (Tansey and Unwin, 1969; Tansey, 1971). Similarly Professor William Taylor led a team which developed a comprehensive simulation based on a hypothetical school 'Severnside Comprehensive'; this was used as the basis of a successful series of TV programmes for teachers in 1969, on Harlech TV.

Since then, the use of simulation at in-service courses for headmasters and prospective headmasters has become widespread; in related fields simulation is used in training youth leaders, social workers (McEachern and Taylor, 1967) and community service volunteers (Dembitzer, 1971).

### The current educational context

It may be worth noting, very briefly, the educational context into which simulation fits. A major impetus in educational thought and practice of this century has been towards the development of forms of learning which have emphasized active participation by pupils. In many classrooms, the informality of group work and of classroom conversation is now an accepted part of the working day, particularly in situations where pupils are learning at different rates, and so are likely to be working on different projects.

Clearly related to this is a renewed study of the function of language in developing and educating the mind. The work of both

Vygotsky and Bruner has suggested that a child's thinking power is not necessarily measured by his vocabulary, and that the development of his thought may well be restricted by insufficient language practice.

As James Britton has written (Barnes *et al.*, 1969):

The domination of lessons (by the teacher's spoken language) seems to amount to an unintended restriction of the kinds of learning that can go on in the classroom . . . It is not that there is too much language, but that it is not fulfilling its functions as an instrument of learning. *Rather, language is seen as an instrument of teaching* (p. 66).

If pupils have chances to reorganize their own perceptions and ideas by discussion (especially with their fellow-pupils) it may not only encourage them to improve their own powers of expression, but also lead them on to grapple with more difficult problems. 'Present talking is future thinking,' as the London Association of Teachers of English put it in their 'Language Policy across the Curriculum' (Barnes *et al.*, 1969).

In a similar way, the Piagetian idea of 'concrete operations' as a stage in child development is itself a preparation for the stage of 'formal abstractions' which is reached at a later time. In the struggle with the operations, the ideas of the subsequent stage are revealed, considered and first shaped.

There is also, in the current climate, an increasing demand from students at all levels for curriculum material which is seen to be relevant to the society in which they live. Bruner's dictum that 'the value of any piece of learning over and above the enjoyment it gives is that it should be relevant to us in the future' represents the feeling that the fruits of a modern-day education should be *seen* to fit needs, sometimes even in the relatively short term. Concern about what is appropriate material to teach pupils staying on until sixteen, now that the school-leaving age has been raised, centres around this point.

This has provided a focus not only for the introduction of new subject material into the curriculum, but also for the development of studies which go across the traditional disciplines. In the humanities, there have been several movements in this sphere, and a number of calls for the design of a curriculum that is problem-based, or, perhaps more realistically, issue-oriented (Storm, 1971).

The world in which these problems have come to the fore is anything but static. The very rate of change is itself a catalyst in the recasting of ideas and the numerous shiftings of viewpoint in education. McLuhan's sardonic comment that the 'expert is the person who stays put' resounds with particular impact on some parts of our teaching strategies and activity.

But not only do we need to be reconciled to change as individuals, we need to find ways to convey and communicate the force and implication of change to our pupils; and to equip them to live in a world in which change itself is a constant.

In relation to these trends, three major attributes of simulation seem significant:

1. It is a technique oriented towards *activity* in the classroom, and in such activity both teachers and pupils participate. It represents an informal and corporate approach to the understanding of a situation.

2. It is usually *problem-based* and therefore helpful in the development of inter-disciplinary approaches to learning. It also frequently involves the use of social skills which are directly relevant to the world outside the classroom.

3. It is a technique which is fundamentally *dynamic*. It deals with situations that change, and which demand flexibility in thinking, and responsive adaptation to circumstances as they alter.

# Chapter 3
# The Advantages of Instructional Simulation

At this stage it seems appropriate to ask what are the strengths that simulation can bring into the classroom. In considering some of the possible advantages (and disadvantages) of the technique, two themes are particularly prominent. One concerns the claimed development of student motivation, and the other relates to the role of simulation in providing relevant learning material.

## Motivational Advantages
### A heightened interest and excitement in learning

Increased student motivation, stemming from heightened interest in the teaching and learning process is a commonly reported phenomenon following simulation exercises. Without doubt, this is the clearest and least disputed gain attached to simulation in the classroom, despite the difficulties of measuring it. It seems to apply at widely differing levels of learning.

This one quality alone is seen by many as sufficient reason for continuing to pursue simulation experiment and development. The body of opinion on this point is uniform and impressive; but *why* simulation arouses and sustains a high level of interest, enthusiasm and excitement, is relatively unresearched.

### The divorce from 'conventional wisdom'

Faced with a simulation situation, each participant often has little previous experience and precedent to support him in such a novel context. Even when the student has had some previous experience of simulation techniques, there is little likelihood that there can be conscious transfer of strategic ideas. Consequently, a level of freshness and novelty is generally maintained.

Thus, few participants are able to approach dynamic simulation experiences with a tool-kit of 'cook-book' solutions that can be used, or even a body of theory. Issues must be treated on their merits, alternative strategies must be devised and attempted, results observed and conclusions drawn, on the basis of direct experience

In such circumstances, often both student and teacher are untroubled by pre-conceived notions; there are few panaceas to be used from the 'conventional wisdom'. At best, simulation becomes a channel of communication for the open-minded, tuning the student in to a new wave-length of learning.

## Removal of student–teacher polarization

Pictures of classrooms from former centuries – and even from this – graphically represent the past relationship of teacher and child: teacher stands on a dais, pointing to board or map with a stick, children sit in rows, apparently attentive and presumably passive, except when called on to answer a question. There is a presumption of a polarization of role between the teacher and the taught.

In recent years, however, we have gone some way towards revising this traditional image. In primary schools particularly, more informal situations have developed, where staff and pupils have become partners in corporate activity. The teacher's function has become more to inspire, stimulate and motivate, rather than to direct, order and judge. And this, in turn, has meant that the teacher has been adapting to accept a less dominant, less intrusive role in the learning process.

Simulations are an aspect of this process and broadly egalitarian in style. Few direct judgements on student performance are required as most simulations are self-monitoring. Opportunities usually present themselves which allow participants to recognize their own progress, or that of the group within which they are working, by various feedback methods.

Students take decisions and then observe their consequences. Their own evaluation of these consequences then influences their future actions. Given favourable progress (positive reinforcement), the student progresses to new challenges; given unfavourable consequences of decisions (negative reinforcement), he is likely to re-evaluate the basis of his decision making.

Thus personal tensions and even antagonisms in the teaching situation are likely to be reduced by such a process of self-monitored learning. The teacher's role may be as interpreter of the simulation, and even as guide, but he does not have to pose as expert or as judge.

*Simulation as a universal behavioural mode*

Children are no strangers to games. The Opies' classic text (1959) emphasized the familiarity of the game world even to the very young; from the days of the nursery-rhyme and classroom-shop, children move within a familiar role-playing, simulating environment.

From this one does not argue that simulations are therefore usable with children of all ages, since there is no guarantee that young children are able to distinguish clearly the worlds of 'reality' and 'make-believe', or that they are able readily to apply consciously insights from one world into another – particularly in relation to cognitive learning.

Nevertheless, it has been found that simulations are usable in the upper part of the primary school to some good effect, and certainly with children of eleven years and over. The worlds of play and of free drama have close relationship with the more structured use of simulation for learning, but the idea of putting oneself in the place of another, seems sometimes easier for children to accept without inhibition than adults.

Fines (1970), writing about simulation in relation to history teaching, made this point:

It has for long been common knowledge that play is really a learning situation in the animal world, among primitive communities and with young children everywhere; furthermore, experiential learning has markedly better results than academic instruction in many fields; but until quite recently no one had explored the possibilities in the higher ranges of education, except for the odd military academy or business school...

Certainly we should be turning our attention to this field ... the use of dramatic role-play in history teaching is often relegated to the position of knock-about humour at the end of term, but it could well be organized into a much more searching learning situation by developing a greater commitment to the dramatic content or to the game element.

Acting-out and role-play procedures are age-old; although when embedded in instructional simulation systems, they are cast in a slightly different mould and they bring together differing combinations of media which make demands upon much of the range of auditory, verbal, visual and manipulative skills of the student. Such 'multi-sensory' stimulation clearly has a large part to play in achieving and reinforcing the impact of the technique.

However, simulations should not over-expose or make vulnerable children who are not equipped to cope with certain group-conflict or public situations, for example, the child who does poorly and who is unable to improve on a performance through a lack of ability, the sensitive student who is acutely aware of the attitudes of his peers, the shy child who is unable to participate in any discussion.

Some viewers of simulations have seen them as therefore dangerous with young children (under the age of ten) and we generally concur with this view. In other areas, it may be pointed out that the sensitive teacher, no less than the sensitive child, should be aware of possible tensions that may build up within a simulation situation and should be concerned to counteract them if it appears that they are incapable of being resolved within the context of the simulation itself.

This point is made specifically by some critics of simulation techniques who are concerned about the undesirability of children competing against each other in simulations where there are 'rival groups'. The simulations, despite replicating real-life situations (for example, in the competition of colonial powers seeking to open up a continent, or of rival companies seeking to maximize profits from manufactures) are seen as unhelpful in educating students towards desirable attitudes and values.

Thus, Tansey (1971) suggests that the essential difference between much American and British simulation development is to be seen in the greater emphasis of competitive simulation material in the North American context. In Britain, he suggests, there is a greater emphasis on cooperation and this increases benefits from the exercise:

A game is a contest and a contest can be won or lost but it is the winning or losing that matters. The world tends to look at people who discuss and analyse games afterwards as boorish.

It would seem, nevertheless, that to ignore competitive elements when they are present in real-life situations, simply means that the simulation is ineffective if it is attempting to recreate a past situation for study.

Where competition is an essential part of a simulation exercise, it seems helpful to suggest that the actual *emphasis* on 'who won' should be discreet or non-existent. Simulations are useful not for equating winning with praiseworthy performances, but for playing and experiencing problem situations. The aim of simulation work must clearly *not* be to produce self-satisfied winners in the way that a casual Monopoly session might do.

### Gains related to relevance and learning
*Learning at diverse levels*

Present information concerning the learning impact of simulation is fragmented and based more on hunch and general impression, than on systematic validated research study. This is partly due to the comparative novelty of the technique and to the fact that authors of evaluation studies are often the originators of the simulation or game under review.

The most substantial programme of classroom simulation evaluation appears at present to have been carried out by the Center for the Study of Social Organization of Schools at Johns Hopkins University, Baltimore. The Centre has an Academic Games programme as one of its major centres of activities, and a team of researchers have produced a number of reports on simulation experiments. These vary from Gili Schild's (1971) study on the influence of games in the school achievement of 500 Israeli children (an indirect effect on attitudes and abilities was noted), to one by Steven Kidder of the emotional arousal and mood changes of students during a game (1971). Some of the Johns Hopkins studies show significant improvement in the learning of facts and concepts, but not all.

Of all validation studies completed in this area, we know of none which suggests that simulation is any *worse* than other techniques in teaching factual material; although the time taken to develop a simulation approach may be longer than an alternative approach. In relation to other skills (analysis, synthesis, interpretation, etc.), the evidence varies and is inconclusive.

There seems to be a special need for studies to consider simulations in a much wider time dimension than has hitherto been used. (We know of no study which has so far measured the effects of classroom simulation in relation to years, rather than months – and yet one of the hoped for results, as Bruner suggests, is the greater embedding of the understanding of structure and process at a deep level in the mind.)

The use of simulations in the classroom often implies a change not only of technique but of objectives in relation to what it is intended the pupils should learn. By their very nature, many simulations would be oblique in teaching factual material; yet it is this which normally forms the basis of 'learning' that is tested at the end of experimental studies. Other forms of learning are less susceptible to research testing procedures.

It should be pointed out that many users of simulation would not wish to evaluate its learning possibilities separately from the other strategies which make up the teaching unit in which it is included. They would argue that the simulation acts as a stimulus to subsequent learning and that this spin-off interest can properly be considered as part of the benefit of the technique, even though it may be developed through more traditional methods of learning.

A number of simulations appear to have been useful with both gifted and slow learners at the same time (Gordon, 1968) and in higher education, inexperienced students and seasoned professionals have also seemed able to learn from each other (Abt, 1968).

It is in this type of learning activity, in our experience, that benefits accrue widely. High flyers are motivated to progress to even greater heights without adverse effect on the less gifted who, in turn, learn from their peers and pursue their own course as fits their inclinations. If simulations involve group decisions (with students simulating the board of a manufacturing company, the government of a country, the editorial team of a newspaper) there is also the possibility of learning not only about the process itself under scrutiny in the simulation, but about the external influences which shape it.

*Decision-making experience*

The group organization of many simulation situations also deepens the understanding of decision-making processes, but it is not an essential ingredient to this.

Even an individual participant in a simulation exercise faces a staged introduction to decision making, although he may be unable to externalize problems in the way in which he would in a group.

Simulation participants need first to demonstrate their ability to understand and then come to terms with their synthetic environment. Often by the gradual increase of data or rule complexity, simulations can be sequentially more challenging and so call decision-making skills into action step by step.

The participant may show competitive, cooperative or irrational behaviour in his appreciation of the situation. The technique brings together not only the student and concrete environmental data, but the vagaries of chance and the effect of human relationships. The participant needs to synthesize all these and yet still see the basic problem in realistic terms.

As the participant thinks for himself about the decisions he may take during the simulation, he also comes to understand the impact and consequence of his own and others' actions. Almost every element or component in the decision-making process can be introduced. Data must be selected and organized. The relevant must be recognized and the trivial dismissed. Strategies must be invented and alternative courses of action on occasion must be planned and implemented. The occurrence of uncertainty must be held in account and cooperation and competition organized and managed.

In these respects simulation is potentially a very flexible and useful framework in which to practise decision making and observe it at work. It can incorporate different levels of decision making, diverse varieties of phenomena and considerable open-endedness.

### Role awareness

Some users of simulation would claim that an important pay-off involved was that of increasing role awareness. To feel what it is like to be in someone else's shoes, and to appreciate some of the ramifications of particular types of behaviour might be considered a more important objective than the understanding of the process in which the behaviour was taking place.

Games such as Project Simile's Starpower in which a change

in attitude is sought, and those with extensive role biographies to be considered before the simulation is begun, might have role awareness primarily in mind. Simulated social systems (e.g. of a local school community or town) might well intend a degree of empathy with some of the roles as a major objective.

It is possible that simulations can develop this situation, although it would seem difficult to fully implement the objective without preliminary study and considerable explanation.

The experience of Clayton and Rosenbloom in using some of the Bruner Social Studies Curriculum Project material may be worth quoting.

... the resultant games combined and confounded the potential of games for role-playing and strategic uses. Role-playing and strategic analysis, rather than complementing each other, turn out to be incompatible behaviours, one requires immersion and loss of perspective, the other requires stepping back and objectivity. This, and a number of other problems have become evident through the classroom trial of educational games....

Students interacting with each other in games do learn something about human behaviour, but what they learn is how other schoolchildren respond to an unfamiliar game, not how Netsilik hunters respond to an approaching caribou herd ... we believe that the fruitful path is to choose games which emphasize strategy and structure rather than personal roles (Boocock and Schild, 1968).

Clayton and Rosenbloom's point about the incompatibility of role play and strategic development may well be an important one to note; it would seem to suggest that a simulation should not attempt to concentrate on *both* potentialities of the technique at once, unless there is ample time to allow both 'immersion and loss of perspective' *and* 'stepping back and objectivity'. The exigencies of classroom time probably mitigate against such a possibility, except in the rarest cases.

### An inter-disciplinary view

Simulation has particular advantages to offer in the way in which it can present an integrated or synoptic view as well as providing a vehicle for free inter-disciplinary communication. If problems are under scrutiny in the simulation, they cannot stop short at disciplinary boundaries, there have to be total approaches to the problems. Human, economic, aesthetic, moral factors, may all impinge in unfamiliar surroundings. And the fact that participants are required to see the world at least partially through eyes other than their own, often helps them to be more explicit and less guarded about what they see.

The inter-connection and inter-dependence of ideas helps to generate a richer group dialogue; varieties of attitudes and points of view are drawn together in group discussion.

### The dynamic framework

Simulation is one of the few classroom techniques which comes to grips with time, be it past, present or future. A large number of time perspectives are possible within a single simulation and the greater the compression of time, the sooner participants are forced to continually acknowledge the dynamics of change.

Sometimes these perspectives are clearly defined so that, for instance, one round equals a three-month or six-month period; at other times, the teacher may develop the time analogy by signalling the passage of days or weeks on a blackboard at regular intervals, as discussion and negotiations drift on. In both cases the realities of actual time are being clearly translated into the constraints of classroom time.

Things 'happen' in simulations as they progress and the snapshot view of the world is difficult to reconcile with the process view that simulation tends to emphasize.

### Bridging the gap to reality

For many pupils in school classrooms, schoolwork seems divorced from the 'real world' in which they are anxious to live. Simulation, with its concrete approach to situations, may well be a major tool in the attempt to bridge the gap between these two contexts.

The participant may have a chance to sample the real world in the simulation and yet he can be observed taking real-world type decisions in a risk-free environment. He is no danger to himself, to others, to expensive resources; he can make his mistakes and learn from them, and perhaps later apply their insights in similar or in relevant real-world contexts.

The very success of a simulation in this sphere can sometimes be its undoing. If students have been highly involved in a situation, the interest of the situation itself may be uppermost in their minds rather than its analogue in reality.

As Shirts (1970) has commented:

... games are vulnerable in a way that textbooks aren't. Because the interaction between participants is genuine, there is a temptation to conclude that the model, the facts, and everything about the game are also genuine.

He goes on to discuss this in relation to war gaming, and the difficulty of seeing the game as something other than a basically enjoyable experience; the same point is reflected in Andrew Wilson's (1968) review of simulation techniques, and in his criticism of their shortcomings.

Shirts (1970) gives an example:

... there is a real danger that games about the black community, which are written generally by persons from the suburbs and are based on a series of unfounded cliches about what it is like to be black, not only encourage stereotyping but create an attitude of condescension towards blacks. More importantly, they can give the students a false feeling that they actually know what it is like to be discriminated against or what it is like to be black. Such games should not be played unless there is extensive input from the black community through talks, films, literature, personal confrontations and discussion...

The bridge to reality, in other words, can be destroyed either if the model itself is a false one, or if there is insufficient attention in linking the simulation experience with the reality on which it is based.

False models are most likely to be used if there is a shortage of models from which choice can be made, and if the user is also perhaps the originator. The need to pre-validate models by careful testing points up the importance of the model builder in this situation. The educator uses his greater experience to develop models for use with students; but if they lose verisimilitude in the interests of entertainment or ease of operation, their guilt in supplying false information is considerable. The seductive powers of simulation can be used for bad purposes as well as good.

In developing simulation as a technique, it is not as contrast to case-study material but as support for it. The belief would be that case-study material used *after* a simulation would be more relevant, more easily comprehended, and more likely to be remembered. But it is no doubt possible that the heady wine of the simulation experience may reduce this to less long-term importance. Without research done in the long term, we cannot know.

## Some reservations

In conclusion, it should be stressed that the case presented so far is a personal view. Though simulation activity is growing fast, it is still in its infancy, has its teething troubles and a restricted amount of experience. As yet there are few discernible simulation results which can be viewed as standard reactions. Clearly, the properties reviewed above do not in themselves validate instructional simulation systems as a whole. Promise still needs to be exploited and tempered with scepticism. We have noted some reservations about the technique.

### The time factor

It is a frequent cry of the classroom teacher, that time is the enemy of progress, and that the introduction of new ideas is seriously hampered by the lack of time available and also because of examination demands. Simulations, however attractive, are time-demanding activities and therefore need to prove of high value to justify a place in the timetable, since their use may cut out other learning.

An examination of the nature of some simulations seems to confirm this problem. Despite the careful development of an analogue to an important process, there may well be a good deal of time spent on apparently inessential activities – filling-up forms, getting people organized into groups, shuffling cards and papers, explaining aspects of the simulation to those who do not understand.

The problem of time bears more heavily in the school than in the college. A teacher with a class for two forty-minute periods a week will think carefully before setting up a simulation; a college lecturer may have a day to develop an idea with a captive audience – or even a period of several weeks in which their energies can be concentrated on the job in hand. Whilst the almost ritualistically defined timetable divisions exist in some situations, it is likely that simulations may be relegated to optional 'after-school' activities or end-of-term diversions.

But not all simulations are elaborate or extensive, and it is likely that simple versions of the technique are more likely to have initial use in a classroom, whatever their crudity in design. Movements towards greater selectivity of material in curriculum, and towards the desire to study material in depth rather than breadth may make it possible for this disadvantage to be less crucial in the future.

## The difficulties of availability and cost

The cost of the most commonly used simulation in urban planning courses for instance, is $120 per kit. Where simulations have not reached mass-production level, there is either a correspondingly higher cost for a custom-built kit or a likelihood of unavailability. Within the material produced so far by curriculum projects for the classroom, there is a certain unreality about cost.

Even where commercial firms have contributed to development costs, prices appear high. A kit on locating an oil depot, developed by Shell in conjunction with the University of Bath Department of Education, has had successful trials and usage in schools, but costs £10; not every secondary school can make that kind of dip into its limited requisitional resources for a single activity. A simpler Environment Game kit, developed (reputedly at a cost of £30,000) by the Coca-Cola Company, costs £3 for relatively simple materials. Such are the economics of kit publishing.

As multi-media publishing develops, it is possible that the economics of such enterprises may change, but there is no doubt at present that some materials price themselves into the luxury class. Users of simulation material who develop or adapt their own material may bat on a much stronger financial wicket; and if a simulation costs only fifty pence or so for materials (however many man hours were spent in preparation) it is more likely to be discarded without regret if unsuccessful.

## Operational problems

The use of simulations in the classroom may be unfamiliar not only to the students themselves, but to the teachers and parents of the students. The initial use of such material may pose problems of logistics, operation and general acceptance.

The development of much informal learning and group activity in the early stages of education has allowed students to adjust to more liberal methods in the secondary school with a minimum of reserve, but it is still possible that the novelty of simulation may cause variations in behaviour which err on the side of either high-spiritedness or inhibition. The strong element of participation which is needed makes this inevitable in some early stages, but it does not seem, in our experience, to be a sustained reaction, if the teacher asserts a moderating role in the situation.

Group-discussion techniques in relation to chairmanship, for instance, may need to be elaborated before the simulation, but the general involvement in the simulation situation is usually a self-regulator away from possible disorder.

Perhaps the bigger problem is for the teacher to exercise suitable management techniques, since at many of the key points in the simulation, he may need to deal quite quickly and clearly with spontaneous problems which are raised by the players. This unfamiliarity with the management role for teachers is something which is the subject of much in-service training in the current decade. In many cases, finding the initial courage to experiment is the largest barrier, and once a simulation has been attempted, other experiments and improvements follow quickly after.

One of the biggest problems may be the classroom furniture. Immovable desks or laboratory benches do not make informal discussion easy; rooms of great size may make it difficult for 'master-plans' or visual aids to be seen effectively by all. Wherever possible, groups should be provided with duplicate copies of material which is to be used for general visual display; otherwise there may well be problems as large numbers of students crowd around material in an attempt to discover information.

It may also be wise to consider the relationship between school and parents. At first sight, and unless forewarned, some parents may find it difficult to appreciate and accept the relevance or intention of classroom simulation. (One senses that drama teachers in schools face similar problems – 'I'm not sending my lad to school just to play-act' said one parent, in an interview

with a headmaster at a school where simulations had been used.)
The results of commercial exploitation of games may have left
the impression that they are nothing more or less than a diverting
entertainment. Judicious display, or even a chance of participation at a parents' evening, may be useful in gaining cooperation
rather than hostility.

# Chapter 4
# Preparation and Operation

Using simulation as a technique in the classroom is not a short cut to easy success. It is a demanding skill which requires considerable effort to be rewarding. Perhaps more harm is done through the misuse of the technique than through not using it at all.

Many teachers may see themselves only as users and not as designers of simulations. Nevertheless, an appreciation of the design factors in simulation immeasurably increases the sensitivity and flexibility with which the technique is used.

For this reason it is worthwhile to consider both the design process of simulations as well as the actual operating arrangements. It will be clear that such description of generalities does not meet every contingency. It may help, however, to reveal some of the underlying principles at stake.

## Selecting the model

Round pegs do not fit into square holes – however perfectly the round peg is made. Likewise some simulations do not fit certain educational situations, not because of their inadequacies, but because they were never designed for use in that situation.

The teacher who uses simulation must have some idea of what it is he wants the simulation to achieve, and, comparably, what the simulation itself is likely to achieve. If the teacher desires students to have a competent mastery of a large number of factual pieces of knowledge, he may not wish to use a simulation in which the design emphasis is on the revelation of basic ideas and general principles.

Broadly speaking, most instructional simulations that involve gaming procedures set out to produce their desired effects through:

(a) presenting a simplified abstraction of the bare essentials of a situation free from trivia and irrelevance (often called the 'background noise');

(b) concentrating on making explicit essential relationships and the fundamental interplay between key roles;

(c) unfolding time at a very much quicker rate than normal so that the implications of action in a dynamic situation can be clearly and repeatedly felt;

(d) allowing students to 'sit in the hot seat' and feel the direct impact of the consequences of decision making;

(e) offering opportunities for collaborative learning on self-directed lines (i.e. learning as much from one's mistakes, and from the mistakes of others as from one's successes).

These objectives tend to be the major type of intention in the mind of simulation designers, but they do not, of course, preclude other objectives – e.g. the learning of factual material – which may well come about through participation in the simulation itself.

The identification of some of the intentions of simulation material is not always reflected explicitly in the material itself. Some simulations are passed on and used because 'they seem to work'; sometimes even the designers themselves are in difficulties when seeking to articulate basic intentions.

But without specified intentions it is difficult for teachers to be sure (other than by intuition) that a particular simulation will meet their purposes. The general lack of guidance in this field has caused some writers to suggest that hitherto choosing a simulation for use has been more an act of faith than a judicious recognition of a model appropriate to the user's specific needs.

This situation has been compounded by the tenacity needed to locate material in this field in the absence of much published material or any coordinating centre of materials. (Hence the attempt partly to remedy this deficiency through the inclusion of a directory of some published simulations in Part Three.)

It is perhaps some cold comfort to reflect that this lack of specification about objectives hinders not only simulation, but education in general.

## Designing a model

If there does not seem to be a suitable simulation available for use (even for use via adaption) then the teacher is thrown back upon the need to begin the design process from scratch.

It is not given to everyone to design successful simulations from scratch at a first attempt, since there are delicate balances of theory and practical application that have to be weighed and considered at every stage; but model design itself is a learning process of some value.

Some would consider that the real value of simulation theory lay in the design process, rather than in any insights gained through the operation of the model (Scarfe, 1971); this seems to assume, however, that simulation experience is accompanied by no conscious discussion or de-briefing of any kind. If the latter does take place, the elements of design can be recapitulated in an altogether more coherent and useful way for a larger number of people.

But there seems to be little doubt in our minds that even when a satisfactory model is not achieved, a considerable insight into the nature of the phenomena under study is achieved by those involved in the design process. Sometimes the model-building process itself is one means of demonstrating to the teacher how little he may know about his own teaching objectives, the value of each academic task, its associated response, and its relationship within the general educational framework. The design process calls for clear thinking in relation to the precise formulation of objectives, and a continuous reappraisal of concepts, assumptions and values concerning classroom learning.

If design work is carried out by teachers and pupils together, students are asked to be explicit about their own conception of the way that 'models' work within the real world. (A sixth form in a school might well be involved in inventing a simple simulation that was to be used with lower classes, for instance). Corporate design of this kind implies that designers already have some initial (though perhaps crude) model ideas and that these can be clarified and improved by operating the model (say of a farming system or of the way a newspaper works – see examples in Part

Two). This then encourages public scrutiny and debate about its relationship with the real-world system.

Having said all this by way of introduction it is to be regretted that other people's comment on the basic steps in game design is so far rare and limited in value. There is a lack of well documented case studies which illuminate the design process and spell out step-by-step guidance on the way in which specific types of simulation have been turned into reality. It is likely that this is because most simulation users have so far concentrated on the *use* of the simulation in a teaching context, rather than on the development or the evaluation of the piece of material which they have evolved.

Simulation design may be an iterative, trial-and-error process. But, as such pioneers as Abt (1966), Gordon (1968) and Boocock and Schild (1968) have pointed out, there are some basic stages in the evolutionary process which can be identified and an appraisal of these now seems appropriate.

## Preliminary analysis
### 1. Problem identification

The first need in simulation design is to determine the purpose of the exercise. The isolation of the purpose is not only a preliminary exercise in self-discipline; it is an essential step in making sure that the needs of the simulation are ordered in terms of priorities.

### 2. Context

Once the purpose is decided, there needs to be the identification of a particular context within which the exercise will take place. Some consideration of the scope of the simulation may be involved in relation to this; a farming simulation, for example, may choose a country, a region, a district or an individual farm as the canvas on which it operates.

### 3. Isolation of component parts of the system

Following this, key elements in the system have to be identified, perhaps quantified and related to each other within the system. This usually requires the identification of the particular institutions or groups which will take their place in the simulation, and the identification of the major variables and decision sequences which appear to govern the balance and momentum of the system.

## Operational modelling

### 4. Resource manipulation

Having set up certain initial objectives and identities, it is now time to explore a series of working arrangements. Two important elements are at stake here. On the one hand there is the target group of students, and the practical resources which are available (size of classroom, time, etc.); on the other hand there is the problem situation which is to be represented – it has its own organizational structure, relationships, motivations and 'pay-offs'.

A careful ordering and deployment of all resources to allow a fusion of both situations is required, and the simulation tailored to what can be credibly staged and achieved.

### 5. Making the model work

With the nature of the resources in mind (see 4), it is possible to try and set about reproducing the dynamic nature of the model – the sequences which will take place as the simulation is made to work.

The preliminary identification of participants and objectives is a foundation for this, but the actual process of developing inter-actions ('rounds in the game') is the keystone of the simulation itself. These interactions may proceed by the choice of participants and a resulting discovery of their actions from some card held by the controller; it may develop through the sequential throw of dice or the reading of random numbers tables; or alternatively it may be a continuous process in which rounds as such are not defined, although the working time of the simulation is seen as an analogy to the passing of real time (e.g. one hour in the class-room representing one day in the newspaper office).

But whatever kind of interaction is decided upon it must fundamentally represent an analogy to the process that the simulation seeks to spotlight; consequently, in many simulations it is a decision-making activity which represents the way in which the simulation moves onwards.

Once this interaction is formulated in some satisfactory and manageable classroom terms, a major part of the work is done. What then follows is the need to formulate sequences of 'How to play' and rule constraints which determine the outer edges of the model. Some of these rules can be built into the model framework.

For instance, in a simulation concerning the building of roads from one place to another, the designer might build in a rule which did not allow the branching of routes. This would not be a rule designed to simulate reality so much as a constraint designed to maintain focus on the central intention of the simulation – the provision of major means of communication. Other constraints in the same simulation – say, concerning the amount of money available for building in any one round (month), or concerning the gradients or curves which the road might use – would be constraints founded in the reality of the situation itself.

Other matters of this nature will probably emerge during the third section of the model design, described below.

## Refinement and testing
### 6. Finalizing of rule systems

Once the model's dynamic and operational constraints have been decided, various rule systems can be developed. These rule systems may reflect directly those in the real world; but there may also be some artificial elements as demanded by the resources available. Clearly, most simulation designers prefer to have a heavy balance in favour of the former kind of rule, so that the framework of the game can be seen to mirror reality whatever the state of the game. The rules should be seen as readily adaptable, rather than as a rigid framework for the game.

Working through a 'How to play' arrangement represents a valuable revision of the basic ideas of the game for the designer; it might also be worth mentioning at this point that rule systems are notoriously dull and unreadable, and should wherever possible be for the benefit of the teacher only.

It is far more likely that a simulation will be successful if the teacher explains the basic ideas of the game to his students and adjudicates, and refers back to points as they arise, rather than if he gives out long lists of somewhat incomprehensible rule-systems for preliminary digestion. Clearly games are best learned through *playing* rather than reading or being *told* how to play them.

In our experience, one recipe for simulation failure is typified by the teacher who walked into a classroom with a well-known packaged historical simulation, announcing to his class that he did not know what the box contained but that together they would no doubt be able to work it all out by reading the rules. Even the basic aim of the simulation appeared unknown, and not surprisingly the rule-reading was not an inspiring first activity without guidance.

## 7. Tuning the model

The final stage in simulation design calls for a 'tuning' of the model in order to achieve good results. The critical eye and experienced designer come automatically to shorten this repetitive period, but there almost certainly need to be some 'dry-run' sessions to see what problems arise.

A run-through of the simulation with a group of friends will help to see immediate problems, before the simulation is launched into the more critical atmosphere of the classroom.

It is important to note, however, that the success of the simulation needs to be seen not merely in terms of its successful operation, but ultimately in terms of its relationship to the real world it seeks to represent. However enjoyable or intriguing the model, it is of little use if it has shifted away from the external realities from which it was originally built.

There is an insidious temptation to build in rules because they seem to equalize the chances of participants, or because they create nicely dramatic situations; this may well serve the purposes of those who build games for commercial entertainment, but it does little to win friends for simulation in an educational context.

Whatever the result, it is essential to be reminded that we are concerned with a partial picture which endeavours to communicate essentials. It should always be accepted that classroom simulations are incomplete dramatizations which offer a bridge between theory and practice.

At the heart of the model-building process are a set of choices that the builder or designer makes at some time or other in the seven steps mentioned above. We list these as choices below, but in fact they could be seen as the representative ends of axes, along which each particular simulation is placed, depending on its purposes.

1. Richness of detail        *v*. Manipulative simplicity
2. Complexity/accuracy       *v*. 'Playability'
3. Logically structured
    learning sequences       *v*. Free player involvement
4. Immediacy (manual
    operation of choices)      *v*. Machine or computer calculation
5. Highly general objectives *v*. Specific objectives
6. Closed system            *v*. Open system (anything may evolve)

In short, the simulation design process is not without both rigour and challenge.

### Simulation operation

With the simulation selected, designed and tuned, it is possible to consider the operation of the technique itself. In doing so, it is vital to see it as part of a total learning sequence and not as an isolated activity to be used in desperation or as a novelty. Some comments about the operational context of simulations are therefore set out below.

### *Introduction and briefing*

The use of simulation in the classroom usually demands at least preliminary briefing and at best a more general introductory period before the briefing.

If full use is to be made of the simulation experience, it is necessary to prepare pupils for it; they cannot fruitfully take decisions concerning, say, an international boundary dispute, if they have no conception of the nature of international boundaries or the rules regularly covering their demarcation. Background information may need to be provided in order for the simulation to be sensibly used; a radio or TV programme may perhaps provide such initial information, or, alternatively, work prepared and provided by the teacher. The simulation itself is probably the key and central part of a unit of work; the core which gives experience from which comes not only interest and stimulation, but spin-off results which may relate back to some of the initial background.

Even if such introductory work is not thought necessary to the needs of the simulation, there needs to be preliminary briefing – such briefing may last anything from fifteen minutes to a whole period in school time. Where corporate design experience has not been a preliminary, the briefing session must assume greater importance.

At least three types of preparation are needed within such briefing sessions:

1. The introduction of the background of the simulation.
2. An introduction to simulation as an instructional mode.
3. Preliminary mechanics to the simulation itself – casting of roles, discussion of the objectives of participants, etc.

It should be emphasized again that the teacher probably needs to provide just as *little* of rule information as he dare.

## Trial plays

An extension of the briefing process may be the 'trial play'. In order to help pupils fully understand the initial mechanics of the simulation, it may be necessary to expose them to a slow-motion trial of the actual procedures which operate during the simulation. Such occasions are the one time in simulation education where the teacher may be seen assuming the 'traditional' role of expositor. He may teach the unfolding sequence of events stage by stage and answer questions that arise concerning the central issues represented, the operational constraints, allocation of time for the exercise, etc.

The 'trial play' is not always necessary, but if it is omitted, teachers must prepare for a first round in which confusions may arise.

## The simulation itself

As with all the stages so far enumerated, there is no one way to present or run simulation exercises. The role of the teacher depends very much on the specific situation, bearing in mind that he or she is on hand in the last resort as a final arbitrator.

But it is clear that simulation as a technique is a child-centred learning situation where unfettered motivation is to be encouraged rather than restrained, and where free exploration and self-discovery at both individual and group level should be maximized.

Therefore nothing in any simulation should be regarded as final or absolute. For example, rule systems should be open to challenge and procedural points can usefully be changed through majority agreement. One of the authors recently took part in a simulation concerning the exploration of the North Sea for gas. Rules were written concerning the development of pipelines in the sea to certain terminals. One group came up with a surprising strategy which demanded a land pipeline and an alternative terminal – neither of which were mentioned in the simulation rules. The teacher in charge dealt with the situation by calculating land pipeline costs on the spot, and by deferring the request for an alternative terminal for two rounds while he thought about it, reasoning that this was an accurate simulation of what a government would do when faced with the same problem! He then authorized the alternative terminal and the group in question went on to work out a satisfactory solution to their transportation problems, despite the period of waiting. Contention and conflict of this sort can be rewarding experiences if properly examined and openly reviewed.

Within the classroom situation itself there can be a rhythm of activity which can mix teaching with group activity. The teacher may use the end of a round or sequence of a simulation as a point at which to emphasize what has happened, or point out a situation; in doing so, he not only integrates orthodox teaching method with the simulation in a creative way, but also, if needs be, retains a hold on the logistics of the classroom situation. Crescendos of noise can be cut off in their prime by the judicious intervention of the teacher, should this be a hazard of the particular situation.

Handling a dynamic situation like this is not without its problems, however, and it would be mistaken to impress too much surface material into the student during the simulation itself. He is more likely to improve his insight and general orientation to the problem than consciously perfect a skill or learn pieces of information.

It may be useful to conclude this section with a check-list of some of the characteristics which may hopefully emerge during the operation of the simulation with students:

1. They may show a perseverance to pursue an understanding of the basic idea in depth before becoming involved in the actual operation.

2. They may show a willingness to develop pre-exercise strategies, and a readiness to modify these in the light of the simulation experience.

3. They may show a sensitivity to critical relationships within the simulation, and to their evolution and change over time.

4. They may show a readiness and ability to make decisions whilst under considerable pressure.

5. They may show openness with respect to intuitive judgements when more reasoned alternatives are not possible.

6. They may show tenacity in the face of disappointing results and a desire to improve performance because of this.

7. They may show a consciousness of the important role or roles and the power of group bargaining and decision-making.

Conversely, of course, they may reveal an absence of these things. Different simulations will show these characteristics up to a greater or lesser degree. But they represent some of the human situations which may arise during simulation activity, quite apart from the spheres of cognitive or affective learning with which the simulation is identified. Thus the social significance of these techniques in the classroom is considerable.

## De-briefing

There must be post-game sessions to put the simulation in proper perspective. The experience gained during the simulation needs to be capitalized upon and focused into consciousness, or else time spent on the experience will have been largely wasted.

The teacher's task here is more clear-cut, and, if the need arises, more dominant. He is on hand to help the participants to review systematically what they have been doing, what they have or have not learnt, and to correlate this with the reality of some situation about which it was hoped they would learn.

It may first be necessary to draw attention to some of the events of the situation from the teacher's perspective and to discuss with the students in the class how these events came about. Such discussion provides not only a revision of the simulation in capsule form, but an alternative interpretation of it. The discussion may also help to clarify the motives and reasonings of different groups in making certain strategies.

From this, it is likely that the teacher proceeds to a consideration of case-studies which seem relevant to the simulation topic. The teacher may indicate how or why certain actions in the simulation seemed at variance with what had happened in real life situations; the discussion of such variances is usually one of the most valuable parts of the task of applying the simulation model back to the actual situation which it seeks to illuminate.

Then may come some kind of de-briefing questionnaire to capitalize on the work done and to provide a referent for the teacher in evaluating the worth of the unit of work which includes the simulation. There may also have been a similar questionnaire administered at the beginning of the unit of work so that a pre-test and post-test comparison can be made.

Another large body of feedback material can come from the examination of monitoring systems (e.g. tape-recording or even CCTV) which enable parts of the game to be played back and re-examined (action-replay in an educational rather than a sports context!). This material may be examined by the teacher alone, or by the teacher and students together, depending on time availability.

There is also the additional evidence that can come from post-simulation reports and comments made by students, whether voluntarily, or possibly as homework assignments. In our experience, students are very ready to make such comments honestly and without reticence.

Although it is not wise to make too many generalizations about the de-briefing process, at least six aspects of post-game discussions can be identified:

1. Initial perceptions of the simulation;
2. The model itself;
3. The operating sessions and their progress;

4. The results of the simulation itself;
5. The learning achievements;
6. Feedback on the whole system, i.e. general reactions to the experience, suggestions and ideas for improving the model and its future use, motivation for further work, etc.

## Curriculum integration

A final word seems appropriate to emphasize further the need to see simulation as but one component in educational development. Few, if any, simulations claim to be sufficient by themselves. However exciting and motivating the operational experience, a good deal of preparation and groundwork must be accomplished beforehand to reinforce the meaning and purpose behind an instructional simulation system. What does seem apparent, however, is that the simulation technique itself is one of great potency, if used properly in this way.

An unvaried diet of simulations is also likely to lead to steadily diminishing returns (just as a non-stop programme of educational films or slide-shows blunts its own virtues). As with any technique, care is needed; simulation may be used efficiently or inefficiently.

Simulation does not offer an automatic set of pay-offs, and the achievement of satisfactory results depends in the last resort not only on the particular 'mix' of human and technical resources, but on the quality of the simulation model and the skill of the teacher in marshalling his resources and channelling them towards identified objectives.

# Chapter 5
# Concluding Remarks

Most of this text has been devoted to a shorthand guide to some of the operational significance of simulation in the classroom. Like any shorthand (and like much instructional simulation) it is an over-simplification designed to communicate a skeletal message. Much remains unsaid; much remains to be researched. By indulging in the realms of 'black and white', some of the shades of grey have almost certainly been overlooked.

But ultimately we have been trying to explore a deeper understanding of the potential and the characteristics of the technique, rather than recruit transitory converts. If in part this text serves as the basis for experiment or as a platform for wider and more enlightened discussion, it will have gone some way towards its limited aims.

We acknowledge a clearly felt need for more discriminating discussion on educational innovation and instructional simulation in particular. The state of the art in simulation today invites comparison with that in programmed learning some ten or fifteen years ago. At that time emotive generalizations for or against the technique abounded. Today they have been replaced by a more specialized and less strident debate on aspects of programmed learning and on the use and value of particular programmes in prescribed settings. We expect a further decade to bring a similar level of discrimination to simulation discussion.

For the moment, progress is certainly retarded by the limited number of educational simulations available in published form in Europe. The situation is somewhat better in the United States but, even there, it is far from satisfactory. Again, the parallels with the growth of programmed learning seem significant. In the early years, a shortage of programmes led to a distorted view of the technique as a whole. The situation was eased by time, energy expended and considerable commercial exploitation of the possibilities. But Zuckerman and Horn (1970) in a recent survey considered that 'simulation gaming is perhaps the fastest growing new method of instruction' and were able to chronicle a mushroom growth in the USA.

If one thing can be learnt from these pioneering developments, it is that generalization should be treated with considerable caution. Today's simulation model may in no way be indicative of tomorrow's range.

It seems important to remember constantly that a great deal has been developed and achieved in a short space of time, but that experience does not extend over a long enough period of time for a 'body of knowledge' to have been accumulated. Even less can one call upon sound theory and principles of practice.

Variations from one simulation to another are not going to be easy to measure, and there is little if any sign as yet of a realistic validation of simulations in terms of the style of learning which they represent.

Nevertheless, systematic review of the wealth of subjective comment from regular practitioners alongside some critical observers' comments seem more than sufficient to encourage further work. Increased and more varied experimentation and trial is obviously vital to efforts of this kind. This does not always imply that new base models need to be designed; a willingness to sequence particular activities in a different order, or to use the simulation in a different context may be a way of improving potential.

Following from this, it may be inferred that the authors consider that simulation has been and continues to be *misused*, even by enthusiasts. The fact that new models are sought with greater vigour than the classroom refinement of existing ones may in some ways reflect the absence of consistent criteria on which to develop such refining processes.

In summary, this text seeks to develop a wider understanding of a new technique through increased experiment and through more enlightened use. Just as greater discrimination is required, so too is improved communication. Many more teachers and students need to be made more aware and knowledgeable of the technology within their grasp. The expertise of the comparatively few has to be more efficiently diffused to the grass roots of the educational system. The impact of 'systems thinking' on educational practice is a likely feature of the decade to come, and within this framework simulation is likely to assume an important place.

Instructional simulation seems to have considerable potential in the classroom, but much work remains to be done if even a small part of this promise is to be properly realized in the immediate future.

# Part Two
# Six Games and Simulations

It would be an impossible task to achieve a complete
cross-section of style and coverage in choosing six games and
simulations to exemplify the discussion in Part One. But the
group of games that follows does cover a wide variety of the
types that are currently being used in the classroom. Each of the
authors has set out some basic information about the game or
simulation under the headings of 'Aims', 'Context', 'Equipment'
and 'Operating procedures'. In three cases the full amount of
material is reproduced, and in the other three considerable
samples of the material. Thus some concrete indication of what
such exercises involve can be judged by the reader.

The Herefordshire Farm Game is a relatively simple and
structured game which introduces some basic ideas about the
process of farming and the decision taking involved within it;
it has been used often in primary schools, as well as at the
secondary level.

Front Page is also simple in style – with an additional constraint
of 'working against time' built into it. Its use is most likely to be
within the English classroom, though, as the author points out,
its aims have a more general significance both in regard to its
principles of operation, and in regard to the discussion of what is
'important' news.

Chemical Manufacturing crosses disciplinary boundaries, and
is a game in which the problems of business economics intrude
on a specifically scientific context. It allows much discussion and
'bargaining' within a simple rule structure.

The Urban Growth model is of a different kind – an example of
the mathematical model in which participants are operators of
processes (through random numbers tables) rather than
continuing decision makers. This Monte Carlo style simulation
seeks to reproduce general patterns, rather than account for
individual events.

Congress of Vienna is essentially an open-ended simulation in
which much background information is provided before open

discussion; 'anything may happen', including a simulated treaty disagreement, or final confusion (war?).

The Conservation Game, like Congress, also takes some considerable time to organize and play and is different in scale from the earlier examples in this respect. Here there are a wide variety of role-briefs to be mastered, and a need to reach a final decision about siting an airport.

All six games and simulations here do not lack classroom experience and testing; all have proved themselves successful in the eyes of a number of teachers who have used them.

# Chapter 6
# The Herefordshire Farm Game

Devised by W. V. Tidswell, Hereford College of Education

## Aims

This is not 'just a game' – but a framework within which children can actively participate to find out more about patterns of land use and choice of crops. It has a distinctive county pattern in this version but can be adapted (for instance) for a tropical region with more pronounced and predictable seasonal rhythms, or for some other area.

More specifically it intends to:

1. Introduce the idea of short-term and long-term cropping (hence the permanent nature of some crops, and the absence of income from woodland during the period of the game);

2. Show how relief may influence land use patterns (woodland on the hilltop contrasts with pasture in the plain);

3. Show not only that weather affects crop yields (see Table 2), but also that there is a chance element beyond the farmer's control (random numbers);

4. Show that human decision determines land use in regions other than those where physical extremes are apparent.

NB – Simplified climatic types are used but resemble English seasons. Soil fertility is regarded as even (modern fertilizers). Traditional crop rotation is no longer current universal practice. The scale of the unit is that familiar in field study.

## Context

The game is used in schools as part of teaching about farming in the British Isles – often as an adjunct to a case-study. It is a fairly simple game and has been used with children aged between nine and fifteen years, and across the whole range of ability.

**Equipment**

Each pupil (or group of pupils, as preferred) is equipped with a worksheet (set out on page 72.) Extra copies of the worksheet are helpful but not essential. Dice may be used to determine weather types if preferred to random numbers.

**Operating procedures**

These are set out in the instructions. The teacher may announce the weather types either by chance, or as he considers useful in the learning situation of which the game is a part (i.e. he may contrive to use the full range of weather types, if felt desirable).

## Exercise sheets for pupils

Mr Brown is a farmer at Canon Pyon and is going abroad for five years. Imagine that you have been appointed to manage the farm whilst he is away. He has instructed you to make as much profit for him as possible and you must therefore plan carefully. He also does not wish you to change the fruit and hop fields whilst he is away. Why? Study the plan of the farm together with the details of fields and crops.

1. The farm is 235 acres in size and is divided into 12 fields.
2. Details of the fields.

### Table 1

| Field number | Area in acres | Crop to be grown |
|---|---|---|
| 1 | 25 | Permanent pasture |
| 2 | 35 | Free choice |
| 3 | 30 | Free choice |
| 4 | 8 | Blackcurrants |
| 5 | 35 | Free choice |
| 6 | 10 | Hops |
| 7 | 20 | Free choice |
| 8 | 25 | Free choice |
| 9 | 10 | Cider apples |
| 10 | 10 | Woodland |
| 11 | 12 | Free choice |
| 12 | 15 | Free choice |
|  | 235 total |  |

3. Each year you may grow any one of the listed six crops in a field labelled 'Free choice' provided that you do not grow the same crop in the same field in two successive years. The crops are: barley, wheat, oats, peas, beans, sugar beet.

*How to choose which crop to grow.* We shall assume that the fertility of each field is the same since Mr Brown is a good farmer and has fed the soils correctly for a long time. The crop yield therefore will depend upon the weather for the year, which we call climate. You may expect any one of four kinds of weather:

1. Wet warm
2. Dry warm
3. Wet cool
4. Dry cool

You do not know how often or when each type of weather occurs (the teacher will tell you after you have chosen your crops).

The income per acre from each crop depends upon the weather and can be obtained from Table 2 below:

**Table 2**

|  | Wet warm | Dry warm | Wet cool | Dry cool |
|---|---|---|---|---|
| Barley | 3 | 4 | 3 | 4 |
| Wheat | 3 | 6 | 2 | 2 |
| Oats | 3 | 2 | 4 | 2 |
| Peas | 8 | 3 | 1 | 1 |
| Beans | 4 | 2 | 2 | 1 |
| Sugar beet | 9 | 5 | 3 | 2 |
| Hops | 12 | 15 | 9 | 9 |
| Cider apples | 15 | 15 | 10 | 4 |
| Blackcurrants | 12 | 20 | 6 | 8 |
| Permanent pasture | 4 | 2 | 4 | 1 |

There is no income from the woodland. Why?

*Example.* If you choose to grow peas in Field 7 and the season is a wet, warm one then your income is

8 (income per acre) × 20 (number of acres) = 160

At the same time from Field 6 growing hops your income is

12 (income per acre) × 10 (number of acres) = 120

*Procedure for the game*

1. Choose the crops for your fields and enter them on the worksheet.
2. Check that you have not broken the rules about the maximum and minimum fields for each crop.
3. The teacher will now announce the weather for each year.
4. Enter the income correctly against each field and add up the total. Enter this total opposite Year I in the small table at the foot of the worksheet.
5. *Repeat for five years* and find the total income for the whole period

*Questions to be answered*

1. Why may you not change the hop and fruit fields during this five years?
2. Why is there no income from the woodland?
3. Look again at the plan of the farm. What do you notice about the distribution of the smaller fields?
4. Why are you not allowed to grow the same crop in every field?
5. What else other than the weather could affect the yield of your crops?
6. When did you (a) make the most profit. Why? (b) make the least profit. Why?
7. What was the mean profit over the five year period?
8. If you knew which kind of weather to expect how much profit could you make in one year? In what areas of the world would you know which kind of weather to expect?

Worksheet for fields and crops each year

| Field number | Year 1 crops | Income | Year 2 crops | Income | Year 3 crops | Income | Year 4 crops | Income | Year 5 crops | Income |
|---|---|---|---|---|---|---|---|---|---|---|
| 1 | Pasture | | Pasture | | Pasture | | Pasture | | Pasture | |
| 2 | | | | | | | | | | |
| 3 | | | | | | | | | | |
| 4 | Black-currants | | Black-currants | | Black-currants | | Black-currants | | Black-currants | |
| 5 | | | | | | | | | | |
| 6 | Hops | | Hops | | Hops | | Hops | | Hops | |
| 7 | | | | | | | | | | |
| 8 | | | | | Cider apples | | Cider apples | | Cider apples | |
| 9 | Cider apples | | Cider apples | | Woodland | | Woodland | | Woodland | |
| 10 | Woodland | | Woodland | | | | | | | |
| 11 | | | | | | | | | | |
| 12 | | | | | | | | | | |
| Total | | | | | | | | | | |

| | |
|---|---|
| Year 1 | Total income |
| Year 2 | Total income |
| Year 3 | Total income |
| Year 4 | Total income |
| Year 5 | Total income |
| | Grand total |

Total incomes each year

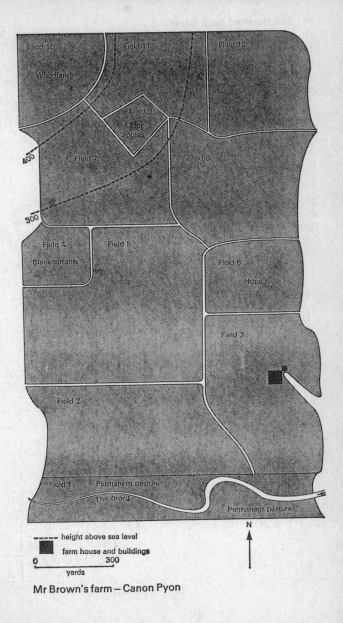

Field 10
Woodland

Field 11

Field 12

Field 9
Cider
apples

400

Field 7

Field 8

300

Field 4
Blackcurrants

Field 5

Field 6
Hops

Field 3

Field 2

Field 1        Permanent pasture
        The brook
                    Permanent pasture

N

- - - - height above sea level
▮ farm house and buildings

0            300
     yards

**Mr Brown's farm – Canon Pyon**

## Teachers' information

*How to determine type of weather.* One method is to use random numbers to determine this. If you wish each of the four types to have an even chance of coming up then use a scale as follows:

| | |
|---|---|
| 00–24 | Wet warm |
| 25–49 | Dry warm |
| 50–74 | Wet cool |
| 75–99 | Dry cool |

This perhaps conveys the variability of British climate.

*Brief extract of random numbers:*

| | | | |
|---|---|---|---|
| 34072 | 76850 | 36697 | 36170 |
| 45571 | 83406 | 35303 | 42614 |
| 02051 | 65692 | 68665 | 74816 |
| 05325 | 47048 | 90553 | 57548 |
| 03529 | 64778 | 35808 | 34282 |

# Chapter 7
# Front Page

Devised by Kenneth Jones

## Aims

Front Page aims to provide opportunities to evaluate materials, think, cooperate, communicate, organize and make decisions in an open-ended situation.

Gaining experience in English skills, and gaining knowledge and ability in the techniques of newspaper journalism are incidental, rather than prime benefits. It is one of a series of seven graded simulations developed by the author.

## Context

The simulation has been used in secondary schools within a variety of situations, and may well fit in with discussion on democratic institutions in social studies, communication skills, information and the media, local affairs, etc. Pupils aged between fourteen and eighteen should be able to cope with the simulation. Participants role-play the job of sub-editors on a local newspaper.

## Equipment

Each group of participants receives:

1. An Editor's memo, complaining about previous errors in the paper, and incidentally setting out most of the procedure for the simulation;

2. A basic 'mock-up' of the lay-out of a front page, showing the position of the lead story, etc., and the possible length of headlines. This is filled in during the simulation, as the sub-editors decide which story goes where, and what the headlines should be;

3. News stories, each consisting of typed paragraphs or 'takes'; each paragraph contains about sixty words and occupies one sheet of paper. (Two days' news intake may be provided.)

There are also Teacher's Notes containing advice on organizing the simulation, and suggestions for follow-up activities.

The Teacher's Notes, Editor's memo, the 'mock-up', and one day's set of news stories, are reproduced on pages 77–87.

## Operating procedures

The participants represent groups of sub-editors for the 'Elham Echo', working against a time deadline in the final period before the paper is printed. They decide the lay-out of the front page, which involves the selection and editing of news stories, and the writing of headlines.

The briefing period consists of reading the Editor's memo, and looking at the sample lay-out and discussing any questions, e.g. should the group operate like a committee or like a real newspaper with a Chief Sub-Editor taking overall responsibility?

The simulation proper is divided into three equal periods of ten or fifteen minutes each. In each period paragraphs of stories can be recorded as having been 'sent to the printers and set up in type'. (It should be pointed out to the participants that it is not possible to leave this until the last period because the printers cannot cope with everything at once.)

In each period the sub-editors receive news stories (from the teacher), and late stories may obviously affect earlier evaluations. The group finally select the make-up of the page from the paragraphs which have been 'set up in type' and write headlines for them. Stories cannot be re-written, but there is complete freedom for selection, for choice of paragraphs, for the order of using the paragraphs, and for the writing of headlines.

Following the 'working period' there is plenty of scope for discussion about the final result and the considerations on which it was based.

### Teacher's notes

In Front Page the participants are sub-editors deciding upon the contents of the front page of their local newspaper, the *Elham Echo*. During the simulation, they receive at different times various news items. They have to decide which items should be used and in which order. Headlines have to be written, and there is a 'deadline'.

Explain to the students that the simulation is open-ended, and that there are no right answers, as such. What matters is how the answers are arrived at.

Most simulations do not aim to teach facts. They are not substitutes for textbooks. Facts about front-page lay-out can best be learned from books about journalism. Nor is the intention to teach specific skills. Front Page is not designed to train students to become sub-editors. The aim is to give practice in general communications skills, employed at a level of adult behaviour.

There is no 'acting' involved. The students do not pretend to be sub-editors. They *are* sub-editors, because they select the news in a realistic situation. This contrasts with passive learning situations in which the students read, memorize and regurgitate.

In the follow-up (de-briefing) the teacher can give opinions on the actions of the participants, but it is advisable to stress that these are opinions rather than rulings of fact. Certainly, both before and during the simulation the teacher should give no hints about attitudes formed in advance about the merits of the news items.

For example, if the pupils show keenness about the story entitled 'Murderer', the teacher should not point out what the Editor's memo says about libel. This question should be delayed until the follow-up.

### How to begin

Read through these notes carefully and examine the material in the simulation before trying to introduce it. Also decide in advance practical questions about the geography of the classroom, equipment required and the allocation of roles. It may be desirable that the slower and less articulate be given the least demanding functions — perhaps keeping a record of the stories sent to the printer. On the other hand, you may feel it unwise to deny these students the chance of responsibility and leadership; on a second run-through there could be a change in functions and the less able could take over, having seen one day's stories go through.

With sixth formers and college students the participants can be encouraged to organize themselves. They could appoint their own Chief Sub-Editor who could have the final decision and who could allocate various jobs, such as headline writing etc. Alternatively, the group could operate like a committee, although it is fair to warn the participants to beware of the time element. If they have not completed the front page by deadline (not one second later) then the paper will go out with blank spaces and the sub-editors might get the sack. With fifth-formers and younger pupils it is advisable for the teacher to allocate some functions to the team, partly to help efficiency and partly to avoid a situation in which one or two participants have tried to take over all the assessment and decision making themselves, leaving the others with nothing to do.

Simulations suffer a great deal less than most school activities from a minority of reluctant students. Involvement is usually considerable, especially when the teacher has explained the nature of the simulation and is thoroughly acquainted with the contents. However, if any misbehaviour or disinterest should occur it is best to deal with it in the context of the simulation.

For example, the participant could be asked to come to see the editor of the *Elham Echo* or to take an urgent telephone call. After a chat with the teacher, the participant could resume the simulation or do something else.

The numbers taking part in Front Page can vary. However, any one team of sub-editors should not be less than four or more than seven. Generally speaking, four or five in the team is better than six or seven. Having arranged the group in the most suitable location available, and with the equipment desired, hand out the 'lay-out' and the 'Editor's memo'. Depending on the age and ability of the students, explain that the 'lay-out' contains four stories of four, three, two and one paragraphs each. Each story has space for one or more headlines. The 'advertisement' is supposed to have been set up in type already, and does not concern the sub-editors. Explain that the 'Editor's memo' was written a few days earlier, and is pinned to the notice board in the newsroom of the *Elham Echo*.

Explain to the participants that the simulation is divided into three equal periods (as explained in the 'Editor's memo') and tell them the length of the periods. Each period should not be less than ten minutes. With thirteen or fourteen year olds it could be fifteen or twenty minutes for each period.

If the teacher wishes to make the simulation easier, the participants can be told that at the beginning of the first period they will receive three news stories, at the beginning of the second period they will receive two, and at the start of the third period one news story. All participants should be shown the sample two-page story 'Industry'. Explain that this story was telephoned in to the *Elham Echo* several days ago, and only the first 'paragraph' was used on the front page. The second 'paragraph' was not used. Explain that all the stories received will contain paragraphs of similar length, and that each paragraph occupies one portion on the lay-out when 'set up in type'.

Refer to the part of the Editor's memo which explains the difference between paragraphs which are set up in type but not used, and paragraphs which are actually used in the newspaper. Emphasize the importance of keeping a record of which paragraphs are 'sent to the printer' in each period, and which are subsequently used on the front page. It is advisable to record this information during the course of the simulation on a form of some kind. The following is an example of how this might be done. Each line is for the recording of one paragraph, with five lines for each period, as not more than five paragraphs can be set up in type during each period.

| Period | Sent to the printer | | Used in the paper |
|--------|---------------------|----------|-------------------|
| | Title of story | Page no. | |
| First | | | |
| | | | |
| | | | |
| | | | |
| | | | |
| Second | | | |
| | | | |
| | | | |
| | | | |
| | | | |
| Third | | | |
| | | | |
| | | | |
| | | | |
| | | | |

Explain that the headlines can be written at any time during the three periods. When they are finally agreed upon they should be written on the lay-out and the title and page numbers of the paragraphs should also be written in. All this must be completed before the deadline.

When the participants are ready the simulation proper can begin. It is, of course, highly desirable that each run-through from the handing out of the first stories to deadline should be a continuous period in the classroom. There are two sets of news stories to simulate two separate days. It is recommended that they be introduced in the following order:

| Period | Firstday | Secondday |
|--------|----------|-----------|
| First | Markets | Pleasure |
| | Murderer | Committee |
| | Playground | Bargains |
| | | Theatre |
| Second | Train | Paintings |
| | Crossing | Stall |
| | | Clerk |
| | | Bulldozer |
| Third | Soccer | Found |
| | | Death |

The procedure is the same for both days. The run-through for the second day is more difficult than the first because there are more stories to select from and because the story 'Found' received during the third period affects the story 'Paintings' which came in the second period. One way of dealing with this would be to use 'Found' which is a one-paragraph story and follow it with paragraphs 2, 3 and possibly 4 of 'Paintings', depending on whether it is the lead story or not.

## Follow up

The follow up should preferably begin with one or more participants explaining the problems, how they were dealt with, and what the final result was. There can be a general discussion on whether, with more time available, they would have reached any different decisions, both in the selection of the stories and the writing of the headlines.

The detailed discussion on what actually happened could be followed by a more general discussion, perhaps dealing with some of the following questions. Should newspapers act as moral censors and omit news items which are unpleasant or unsavoury? Should a newspaper give preference to 'good' news rather than 'bad' news, or should the criterion be news value and interest? If a newspaper decided to give only 'good' news, would its circulation increase or decline? Would it be a good idea to have all newspapers controlled by the Government?

Front Page could also be used as a starting point for other activities on similar lines. It might stimulate the production of a class or school newspaper, or an analysis of actual front pages, or visits to newspaper offices.

**Elham Echo Memo**

From: The Editor

To: All sub-editors
Date: Wednesday 10 March

It really is not good enough. We can't blame the shambles of yester-
day onto the new members of the staff. It is up to the older members
of the News Department to explain to newcomers how we run our
paper.

In order to avoid any more disasters, let me set out a few basic
facts, which should always be borne in mind.

Elham is a medium-sized city and we have many readers because
the *Elham Echo* is published every day of the week (except Sundays)
and contains important news and interesting news about our city
and the area around.

The front page is always left to the last because it is supposed to
contain the most important, interesting and up-to-date items of
news. The news must mean something. (Don't let me hear anyone
else say 'I didn't understand it, but I thought it might be important').
If you don't understand it neither will most of our readers.

Remember what we are not. We are not a trade journal and we
don't want a lot of technical details on the front page. We are not an
advertising agency – if people want adverts then let them pay for
them. We are not a gossip shop – if we print anything which lowers a
person's reputation in the opinion of society generally, then that's
libel and we could be sued for damages. We are not children – we
don't have to believe what people say, even if they are persons of
importance.

Remember what we are. We are a newspaper, and news is what
we are concerned with, not history (although history can sometimes
be news). We must present news fairly, and we must use our common
sense. For heaven's sake read each item twice.

Because of complaints from our reporters do not re-write one
word of their copy. Either accept it or reject it, but don't alter it.
However, you can alter the order of the paragraphs of a story if you
want, and a paragraph from one reporter's story could be added to
another story if it makes sense.

The headlines are entirely your responsibility, and please, please,
check the length of each headline. The printers have been complaining about this, and they are quite right.

Please bear in mind that 8–12 means a headline of eight or nine or
ten, or eleven, or 12 units. It is no good sending down a headline
of thirteen units, or seven, as being 'nearly right'.

Remember that each letter is one unit, each space is one unit, and each punctuation mark is a unit. The headline BIG FIRE LOSS is thirteen units because it includes two spaces. The headline 'TRAGIC LOSS' SAYS MAYOR would be twenty-four units, as it has two punctuation marks, three spaces and nineteen letters.

Play fair with the printer. You know that he can't cope with all the front page copy in the last fifteen minutes before deadline. Divide the run-up period to deadline into three parts, and send no more than five paragraphs in any one period. You need only ten paragraphs for the front page, but it does not matter if an extra five are set up in type but not used. It is better to do it this way than trying to overwork the printer at the last moment.

Finally, remember that the *Elham Echo* is a good paper, and that's why people read it. Keep it good. It's up to you.

# ELHAM ECHO

| Headline  8–12 | 3 headlines each 5–10 |
| --- | --- |
| Second headline  20–30 | |

| 1 | 4 | 2 headlines each 10–15 | 1 |
| --- | --- | --- | --- |
| 2 | 1 headline 10–15 | 1 | 2 |
| 3 | 1 | 2 | 3 |
| | Advert | | |

**Rough lay-out**

## News stories for day 1

*Markets 1*

There was a brisk trade in pigs at Elham weekly cattle market. Dairy cattle were also in demand, although dealings were somewhat fewer than in the previous week. There was a steady trade in sheep and poultry. One dealer said, 'Business is fairly normal for this time of the year. It is much the same as it was last month.'

*Markets 2*

Dealings at Elham cattle market were interrupted by a lion which had escaped from a travelling circus. The lion ran into the market from Brickly Road, but was quickly captured by Mr Potter, a sheep farmer, who pushed it into an empty crate, and fastened the door. Mr Potter said afterwards 'I didn't have my glasses on, and I thought it was one of the sheep.'

*Markets 3*

At Elham town market there were good prices for apples. Most fruit was in demand. Greens were in better supply due to the improvement in the weather which had helped the picking. Potatoes were also plentiful. The price for imported tomatoes was down on previous weeks. The demand for vegetables was generally good.

*Train 1*

The London to Edinburgh express has crashed two miles south of Elham. It became derailed as it emerged from Longtree tunnel, and ploughed across a field. At least thirty passengers have been taken to Elham Town Hospital, but none of them were seriously injured. A hospital spokesman said 'It is a miracle that no one was killed.'

*Train 2*

A railway inspector at Elham, Mr Tom Marsh, said the express had been slowed by a signal just before the tunnel, and had been travelling at about 20 m.p.h. when it came off the rails. The engine stopped about ten yards from a block of flats. All the carriages remained upright, except for the last carriage from which most of the injured were taken.

*Train 3*

The uninjured passengers were taken by coach to Grantham to continue their journey northwards. One of them, Mr Pegley of Edinburgh, to d our reporter 'It seemed as if the train had square wheels. We held on until the train stopped. It was lucky it did not run right into the block of flats.' Railway officials are investigating the cause of the accident.

*Train 4*

A British Rail spokesman at Elham has congratulated the emergency services on the speed and efficiency with which they came to the rescue. Regarding the clearing of the track, he said it would take about two days before normal working was resumed. However, delays would not affect main line traffic, as the main up-and-down tracks are again in operation.

*Playground 1*

The children's playground at Little Mill Lane in North Elham is now a much better place for the youngsters than it was last week. During the weekend workmen erected two new swings. There are now twelve swings in the playground, as well as the slide and roundabout which were built when the playground opened five years ago.

*Playground 2*

A member of the Parks Committee, Mrs Mells, told our reporter 'I do think the children should have somewhere to play. They will grow up to be our future citizens. The council spends a lot of money each year for flowers for the parks. A good display of flowers is very attractive, and if people stopped dropping litter the parks would look even better.'

*Playground 3*

Mrs Mells said that she had served on the Parks Committee for more than twelve years. She said 'I know this is not a record. Some of my colleagues have been on the Committee for nearly twenty years. I suppose that they have got used to it, and feel they are serving the community. After all, that is what really matters today, a sense of service.'

*Playground 4*

Asked if she had any interests in other fields, Mrs Mells said 'I am very keen on welfare work, such as looking after old people. Some of them lead a lonely life, and it is up to us to do what we can for them. That is why I hope you will print all this in your newspaper. I feel it is your duty to print the good things, not just the bad things.'

*Murderer 1*

There is a murderer in Elham, but the police are afraid to arrest him.

This information was given to an *Elham Echo* reporter by Mrs Rita Spin of 6 Grey Road, Elham. Mrs Spin told me, 'Two people have been murdered in the town in the last three years. I know who the murderer is. It is my next door neighbour, Mr Cecil Tellison.'

### Murderer 2

Mrs Spin explained to me how she had discovered the criminal. She said 'Mr Tellison pretends to be an architect. But I know he goes out at night and murders people. He is shifty. He never looks at me. That is because he knows that I know that he is a murderer. It is up to the police to deal with people like that.'

### Murderer 3

I asked Mrs Spin if she had told the police about Mr Tellison. 'I have been three times to the police station,' she said 'but they will not listen to me. They are afraid of what Mr Tellison might do to them. He has guns in his house and rifles and dynamite. I sometimes hear him through the wall pushing a box of dynamite under the stairs.'

### Murderer 4

Mrs Spin also told me that the Chief Constable of Elham, Mr Gerald Sprabley, is in the pay of criminals. She declared 'I know for a fact that he is taking large bribes from the criminal element in Elham.' Mrs Spin also said that the Mayor of Elham, Mr Hoope, is a drug addict who has been paying hush money to the police to keep this secret.

### Crossing 1

About fifty mothers pushing prams and carrying placards held up traffic at Swift Corner in Elham by crossing and re-crossing the road. They were demanding greater safety measures for children who have to cross Swift Corner on their way to school. Two school children were injured there last week.

### Crossing 2

Mrs Vera Uttley, one of the mothers, told an *Elham Echo* reporter, 'Cars wizz round this corner from Blackwell Road, making it very dangerous for the children. We want warning signs put up and a pedestrian crossing. We want the Town Council to appoint a road-crossing warden to look after the children.'

### Crossing 3

Commenting on the demonstration by the mothers, a member of Elham Town Council, Mr John Havery, told our reporter 'It is up to the mothers to look after their children, and to see them safely across the road. The mothers should also see that the children know the Highway Code. Why should the rate-payers have to pay for wardens when it is the mothers who are responsible?'

## Crossing 4

A police spokesman said the question of warning signs and a pedestrian crossing will be considered. He suggested that parents and teachers should get together to draw up a list of people who would take it in turn to shepherd the children across the road. He said the idea of a crossings warden would be discussed by the Council's Road Safety Committee.

## Soccer 1

Elham United have been promoted to the Second Division. They won their final game of the season against Corby Rangers by three goals to two, giving them a one point lead at the top of the table. The match ended in scenes of tremendous excitement, with hundreds of Elham supporters swarming onto the pitch to congratulate the team.

## Soccer 2

United's inside forward, Jimmy Shocken, who scored all three goals, was carried shoulder-high from the field by his team-mates. His last goal, scored one minute before the end of the match, was a brilliant shot inside the near post after having beaten three Corby defenders in a run from the half-way line.

## Soccer 3

Jimmy Shocken said afterwards 'It was great. We have a great bunch of lads.' He said there was no truth in a rumour that he was thinking of asking for a transfer to a First Division club. The Mayor of Elham, Mr Henry Hoope, who is also Chairman of Elham United, said 'We are thinking of giving the team a civic banquet.'

## Soccer 4

The promotion of Elham United to the Second Division means that the plans for a new stand at the Canal Road end will now go ahead. It will cost about £90,000 and should be ready for the start of the new season. This is the first time that Elham United have ever reached the Second Division. They have been in the League for thirty-one years.

# Chapter 8
# Chemical Manufacturing
Devised by David Wilson, Manchester Grammar School

### Aims

These are twofold:

1. To emphasize the inter-relatedness and interdependent nature of the chemical industry;
2. To point out that in the real world the success of a process depends on its profit and not on its chemistry.

The game is not intended to focus on the processes themselves.

### Context

This appeared to be an area of chemistry suitable for simulation treatment. It has been used as part of an optional course on industrial chemistry, with boys of fifteen years of age. The course deals in turn with the historical, economic and social aspects of chemistry, and the game helps to round off the second and introduce the third of these.

### Equipment

Eleven Process Cards are needed and may be duplicated if players number more than this. These comprise Coal (see example), Zinc (see example), Sulphur, Brine, Oil, Vegetable Products (Extractive Industries) and Plastics, Detergents (see example), Chlorine (see example), Ammonia and Hydrogen (Processing Industries). Tokens are needed to represent money (in thousands of pounds) and goods, and perhaps racks to hold these. There are also four Spinners (for 'Buying from Bank', 'Selling to Bank', 'Research and Development' and 'Hazards') (see examples) which can be made simply from cards and pins. A Ready Reckoner will help the calculations of the Bank, and a Flowsheet of processes (see example) will help all groups.

### Operational procedures

The object of the game is to operate the processes on the cards in such a way as to make a profit.

*Preliminaries.* One player (or group of players) is designated as banker. Money is shared out equally amongst players, the bank counting as one player. Any surplus money and the goods tokens are placed to the Bank. The banker then deals a 'process' card to each group, more if there are extras available. Players are then given five minutes to familiarize themselves with their own process (are they extractive or productive?), and to establish who their suppliers, customers and competitors are.

*Play.* This begins by the banker announcing 'open'. Groups act as follows:

Extractive Industries (e.g. Oil) buy goods tokens from the banker, paying the price on the back of their card (plus or minus what the Bank spinner determines for each transaction) *or* buy goods from other players.

They sell these to the processing industries which require them (e.g. Detergent) for the best price that they can get.

Productive Industries (e.g. Chlorine) buy tokens from other players necessary to produce their product. When they have enough tokens to manufacture they can sell to the Bank at the price marked on the back of the card (plus or minus what the Bank spinner determines).

The Bank buys and sells only at the prices on the product card. Having bought or sold, the appropriate spinner is given a turn to determine the *next* transaction. Only one commodity may be bought or sold at a time, and, having transacted one piece of business with the Bank, a player must 'go to the end of the queue'. The Bank only sells or buys where 'extract' or 'public' is shown on the cards.

Players are free to bargain with each other in any way which is allowed by the teacher. Where the Bank is *not* involved, prices shown on the cards need not be used – they are provided only for initial guidance.

Strategies may be discovered by experience. For instance, it may be permissible to sell short, buy futures, corner markets, form price rings and monopolies, force people out of business. mortgage, lend and receive interest, sell businesses or receive commission on this, rent out a process, go bankrupt.

*Vouchers and spinners.* Free vouchers are issued as indicated, given by the Bank to Sulphur and Ammonia only. The Bank price spinners are used with each transaction. The hazard spinner is used as and when the main spinners indicate – and it affects the *following*, not the present transaction. One spin on research may be bought when a commodity is sold to the Bank, or bought; the commodity in which the research is done need *not* be the same as the one being sold or bought.

*End of play.* At a pre-arranged time (say one and a half to two hours after the start?), all transactions stop. By this time there may well be three or four major combines formed from agreements between players (comparable to the modern chemical industry). It may be interesting to see who has most assets in goods, cash and value of process.

Here is the result of one two-hour game:

| Player | Number of industries owned | Profit (£000s) | Main strategy |
|---|---|---|---|
| 1 | 3 | + 2600 | Cornering market and vertical integration |
| 2 | 2 | + 1900 | vertical integration |
| 3 | 1 | + 1875 | |
| 4 | 1 | + 1875 | Syndicate |
| 5 | 1 | + 1875 | |
| 6 | 1 | + 1875 | |
| 7 | 3 | + 1075 | Vertical integration |
| 8 | 1 | + 530 | Research and development |
| 9 | 0 | + 200 | Company 'agent' |
| 10 | 1 | — 190 | Bad luck with spinner! |
| 11 | 0 | — 220 | |
| 12 | 0 | — 230 | Admitted to poor bargaining |
| 13 | 0 | — 245 | |
| 14 | 0 | — 250 | |

Discussion after the game may raise the matters of the ethics of capitalist industry, and the desirability of seeing industry as a related whole.

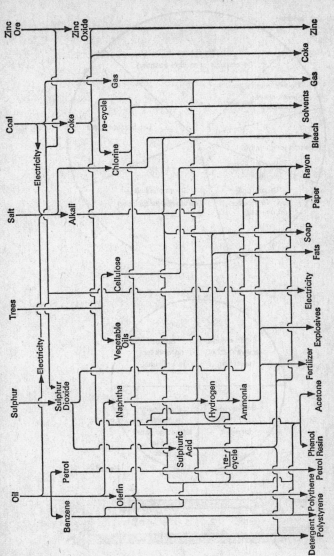

Process diagram — to be given to all players

91

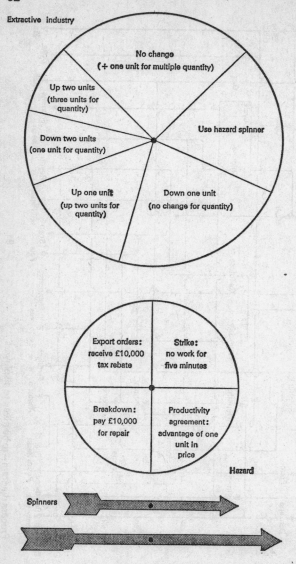

Extractive industry

No change
(+ one unit for multiple quantity)

Up two units
(three units for
quantity)

Down two units
(one unit for quantity)

Use hazard spinner

Up one unit
(up two units for
quantity)

Down one unit
(no change for quantity)

Export orders:
receive £10,000
tax rebate

Strike:
no work for
five minutes

Breakdown:
pay £10,000
for repair

Productivity
agreement:
advantage of one
unit in
price

Hazard

Spinners

Spinners used during the game

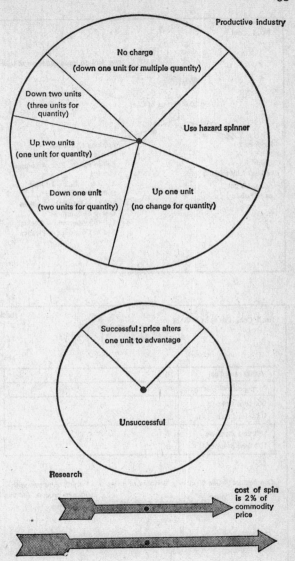

Productive industry

No charge
(down one unit for multiple quantity)

Down two units
(three units for
quantity)

Use hazard spinner

Up two units
(one unit for quantity)

Down one unit
(two units for quantity)

Up one unit
(no change for quantity)

Successful: price alters
one unit to advantage

Unsuccessful

Research

cost of spin
is 2% of
commodity
price

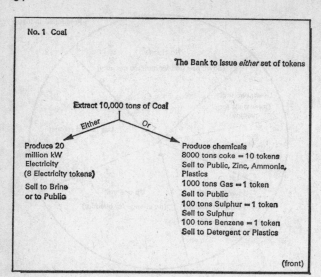

No. 1  Coal

The Bank to issue *either* set of tokens

Extract 10,000 tons of Coal

*Either* / *Or*

Produce 20
million kW
Electricity
(8 Electricity tokens)

Sell to Brine
or to Public

Produce chemicals
8000 tons coke = 10 tokens
Sell to Public, Zinc, Ammonia,
Plastics
1000 tons Gas = 1 token
Sell to Public
100 tons Sulphur = 1 token
Sell to Sulphur
100 tons Benzene = 1 token
Sell to Detergent or Plastics

(front)

No. 1  Coal  Prices in £1000s                               (back)

| | |
|---|---|
| 10,000 tons Coal | 70 |
| 20 million kW Electricity | 75 |
| 800 tons Coke | 50 |
| 1000 tons Gas | 25 |
| 100 tons Benzene | 5 |
| 100 tons Sulphur | 5 |

Competitors:  Oil: Electricity, Benzene, and Naphtha (which competes with
Coke to produce Ammonia)

Public + Zinc; Sulphur

Front and back of Coal process card

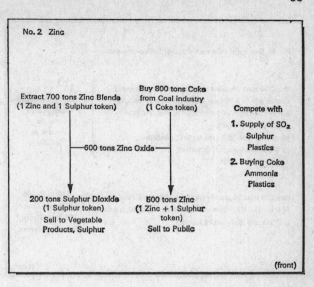

No. 2 Zinc

Extract 700 tons Zinc Blende
(1 Zinc and 1 Sulphur token)

Buy 800 tons Coke
from Coal industry
(1 Coke token)

Compete with

1. Supply of $SO_2$
   Sulphur
   Plastics
2. Buying Coke
   Ammonia
   Plastics

——600 tons Zinc Oxide——

200 tons Sulphur Dioxide
(1 Sulphur token)

Sell to Vegetable
Products, Sulphur

500 tons Zinc
(1 Zinc + 1 Sulphur
token)

Sell to Public

(front)

No. 2 Zinc  Prices in £1000s

(back)

| | |
|---|---|
| 700 tons Zinc Ore<br>800 tons Coke | 40<br>5 |
| 200 tons Sulphur Dioxide<br>500 tons Zinc | 6<br>45 |

Competitors for Coke buying: Public, Ammonia

for Sulphur Dioxide supply: Sulphur, Coal

Front and back of Zinc process card

No. 8  Detergent   Operate either or both processes

Buy 200 tons Benzene from Coal or Oil (2 tokens)
Combine with 400 tons Olefin from Oil (4 tokens)
Sulphonate with 300 tons $H_2SO_4$ from Sulphur
(1 token, 1 voucher)
Neutralize with 200 tons NaOH from Brine
(1 Brine and 3 Electricity tokens)

> Sell 1000 tons
> Detergent to
> Public
> Present all
> tokens

Buy 800 tons Vegetable Oils from Vegetable Products
(4 tokens)   Hydrolyze with 200 tons NaOH from Brine
(1 Brine and 3 Electricity tokens)

> Sell to Public
> 900 tons Soap
> 100 tons Glycerol
> Present all tokens

(front)

---

(back)

No. 8  Detergent   Prices in £1000s

| | |
|---|---|
| 200 tons Sodium Hydroxide | 27 |
| 800 tons Vegetable Oils | 60 |
| 900 tons Soap | 90 |
| 100 tons Glycerol | 10 |
| 200 tons Benzene | 10 |
| 400 tons Olefin | 8 |
| 300 tons $H_2SO_4$ | 6 |
| 200 tons Hydroxide | 27 |
| 1000 tons Detergent | 60 |

Competitors for Olefin, Plastics and Chlorine: for Benzene, Plastics;
for $H_2SO_4$ and Hydroxide, numerous

Front and back of Detergent process card

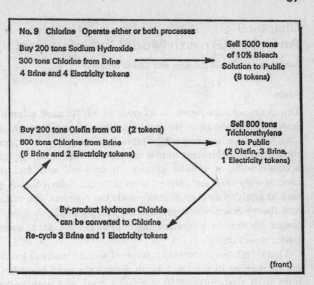

No. 9 Chlorine Operate either or both processes

Buy 200 tons Sodium Hydroxide
300 tons Chlorine from Brine
4 Brine and 4 Electricity tokens
→
Sell 5000 tons
of 10% Bleach
Solution to Public
(8 tokens)

Buy 200 tons Olefin from Oil (2 tokens)
600 tons Chlorine from Brine
(6 Brine and 2 Electricity tokens)
→
Sell 800 tons
Trichlorethylene
to Public
(2 Olefin, 3 Brine,
1 Electricity tokens)

By-product Hydrogen Chloride
can be converted to Chlorine
Re-cycle 3 Brine and 1 Electricity tokens

(front)

(back)

No. 9 Chlorine Prices in £1000s

| | |
|---|---|
| 200 tons Sodium Hydroxide | 27 |
| 200 tons Olefin | 4 |
| 300 tons Chlorine | 15 |
| 500 tons Bleach | 45 |
| 500 tons Solvent | 25 |

Competitors for Olefin, Plastic and Detergent: for Hydroxide, numerous

Front and back of Chlorine process card

# Chapter 9
# An Urban Growth Model (based on Bristol)

Developed by David Gowing and Sheila Jones

## Aims

Ten years ago the work in schools which focused attention on towns was confined to the final chapter of a regional geography text. Site, situation and major manufacturing industries were the most common elements in this description. But urban geography is undergoing a radical change in outlook and techniques; morphology is of less interest than process; description is giving way to analysis as quantification aids the construction of models and theory from which predictions can be made. A town is no longer viewed as a unique phenomenon, but as a source of patterns and trends.

This simulation exemplifies some of the innovative ideas which are happening in the teaching of geography, and has been used both with sixth-formers in a girls' school and with college of education students.

It is intended to:

1. Illustrate the technique of simulation as a predictive tool in planning and in geographical research;

2. Show the difficulties involved in the making of such forecasts;

3. Introduce stochastic (chance) elements as a balance against the deterministic bias of former statements. The chance element may include the complex interaction of variables which as yet we are unable to isolate but it also includes the 'irrationality' of the individual's decision-making processes. These elements can be built into the exercise by using random numbers to generate the growth pattern. It is this procedure, explained below, which constitutes a 'Monte Carlo' type of simulation.

4. Show the strengths and weaknesses of theoretical models. For instance, working on a *past* simulation of growth, 1921–61, enables a predicted pattern to be held up to reality; discrepancies may be seen to be due to the crudity of inputs, the incorrect weightings of variables, or even their total omission. The latter may be characteristics of that uniqueness which once dominated

the approach to the study of cities. One inherent crudity in the model is the assumption that the total growth of population is peripheral – this hides possible cross-currents of migration and re-housing. The refinement of the model, (e.g. with grid squares at a smaller scale, with greater random number choices) might produce a pattern closer to reality, but it is important to note that 'reality' is only one possible growth pattern. Because of the chance element in the random numbers, groups working with exactly the same cell totals will produce different patterns, of which some will be more like what has actually happened than others.

5. Apply a quantitative assessment to the factors affecting urban growth to emphasize their unequal effect. For example, if the desire to be close to the city centre is considered of greatest significance, this factor should not only receive a value higher than that for other factors but also have a gradient of values which decrease from the city centre. Where such gradients seem to occur a series of concentric circles or parallel bands can be drawn on to the map to assist in calculating cell values.

The original version of this model was also intended to encourage an interest in the processes of change which were specifically going on in Bristol – the local area in this case. Bristol is a large area to handle with this technique, and consequently the number of people per unit (1000) is large. Teachers working with smaller urban centres can have smaller numbers, greater base map detail, and thus more refinement. The adaptation of this model to a town in the home region may well be desirable.

## Context

The exercise derives from a similar style of Monte Carlo simulation worked out at a teachers' seminar at Madingley, Cambridge in 1967, designed by D. E. Keeble (see 'School teaching and urban geography', *Geography*, January 1969).

It was included in an urban studies course with first-year sixth formers taking 'A' level who had already done some field work and practical work connected with urban studies in Bristol. This exercise was used to conclude the course.

Similarly, it was used by college of education students in a first year course devoted to urban geography and local studies, and was integrated into field work activities.

**Equipment**

Each student, or group of students working the simulation needs to be provided with a base map of Bristol (derived from the 1922 1″ O S sheet) on which has been drawn a one-kilometre grid. The base map should show the 1922 settlement pattern in outline, and some information concerning relief, drainage, communications and permanent open space.

Each group is also provided with the following set of statistics:

| | 1921 | 1931 | 1941 | 1951 | 1961 |
|---|---|---|---|---|---|
| City and county of Bristol | 384,081 | 397,012 | | 442,994 | 437,048 |
| Continuous built-up area of adjacent parishes (UDs of Filton, Kingswood and Mangotsfield) | 24,499 | | | 48,587 | 66,443 |
| Adjacent parishes | 20,133 | | | 32,939 | 53,633 |

Figures adapted from Census tables

**Operating procedures**

Each group of students is asked to use the base map to produce a map of the growth of Bristol, based on the use of a mathematical Monte Carlo simulation procedure as explained below.

1. Discuss factors which may have affected the shape and area of the city between 1921–51. This is an important part of the total set of procedures. If necessary, refer back to the 1922 O S map and extract further information to add to the base map provided.

2. Consider each grid square in turn, and its potential for development. This can be quantified by drawing up a general table of values for the advantages and disadvantages discussed in 1. e.g. Advantages might be thought to include:

(a) Nearness to main road,
(b) Nearness to a railway station,
(c) Distance from city centre (proportional),
(d) Nearness to open spaces, etc.

Disadvantages might be thought to include:

(a) High relief, or steep slopes,
(b) Land liable to flooding,
(c) Nearness to railway lines, etc.

Each undeveloped or partially developed square should then be allocated an overall score which identifies its potential for development in the view of the group. Cells totally built-up score zero. The value of the cell is obtained by adding together the values quantified for separate factors. (Different groups are likely to evaluate and weigh advantages and disadvantages in different ways.)

3. On a copy or tracing of the matrix (the system of grid squares) list the values decided for each square.

4. Convert these values into random numbers by a process of accumulation. e.g.

| 001 | 006 | 004 | 002 | 000 | 001 | 002–007 | 008–011 | 012–013 | 000 |
|-----|-----|-----|-----|-----|-----|---------|---------|---------|-----|
| 003 | 005 | 005 | 000 | 001 | 014–016 | 017–021 | 022–026 | 007 | 027 |

Value for each square                   Accumulated values
(probability matrix)                     (random number matrix)

5. Calculate the total population growth in the area between 1921 and 1951. Let 1000 people be equal to one unit. The gross density of population in this area is about twenty people per acre, which thus limits the maximum population of an unused square (640 acres) to 13,000 people (thirteen units).

If a cell already has a proportion of settlement estimated at 6000 people in 1921, it can take a further seven units of population.

Mark on the tracing the number of population units *already* present (as estimated) in 1921.

6. Simulate the growth 1921–51 by using random number tables. Pick out series of three digits from the tables. Where these figures appear on the map (see 4) assign a unit of population to the grid square in which the figure occurs. Mark the square on the tracing with an X for each unit assigned.

Where the numbers do not appear on the map (e.g. 926 may not appear since the accumulated values may not reach that high) or where the square is *already full* (from previous Xs) the random number is discarded.

Continue the simulation until the number of Xs equivalent to the 1921–51 growth have been reached in each of the three areas.

7. Use the information derived from the grid tracing (i.e. the Xs) to plot the projected area of the city 1921–51 by simulation.

8–14. Repeat procedures 1–7 for the period 1951–61, assuming that factors affecting growth may have changed from those operating in the earlier period.

15. Compare the 1921–51 and 1951–61 growth patterns with the Seventh Edition of the 1″ O S map of Bristol, published in 1963.

Compare the different results produced by groups. Discuss what accounts for the differences. This discussion is vital to the whole exercise.

In the stages of the allocation of new populations, logically, each X assigned changes the spatial pattern and subtly affects further growth. It is impracticable to accommodate this in a model designed for school use, but the breaking of the simulation into two stages does partly allow for this.

For example, in the local Bristol context, the post-war era of planning recognizably created a different relationship between Bristol and its neighbouring counties; the Somerset boundary became a rigid barrier to the city's expansion. Through planning controls, densities were lowered to nearer seventeen people per acre.

It may also be felt that in the second stage of the simulation there should be different values for distance, since the increasing affluence and mobility of the population has created a very different perception of distance, whether measured by mileage, money or time. The suburban railway has also become both relatively and absolutely of less importance.

## Simplifications

If it is desired to simplify the above model still further, the following adaptations can be made.

1. Reduce the model to a *one*-stage simulation, 1921–61.
2. Work with a *gross* change in the three populations (128,411) and ignore the need to have certain increases in certain areas.
3. Increase the X value to a larger figure (e.g. 5000 – which would reduce the number of allocations from 128 to 26). Allocation of random numbers is one of the most time-consuming aspects of the model and not the most valuable part of it.

All these modifications have the effect of making the model less refined but they may make the exercise more suitable for use in a situation where the time allocation is limited.

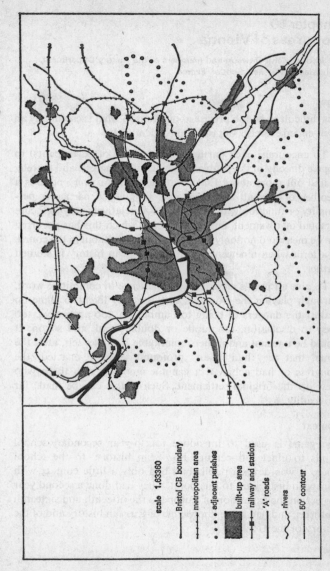

**Bristol 1921**

scale 1:63360

— Bristol CB boundary
••• metropolitan area
•••• adjacent parishes
■ built-up area
■—■ railway and station
— 'A' roads
∿ rivers
— 50' contour

# Chapter 10
# Congress of Vienna

Devised by Keith Dawson and members of the History Department, Haberdashers' Askes' School, Elstree

## Aims

It is difficult to be too precise about aims in what is essentially an open-ended exercise, but two can be identified:

1. To encourage each participant (or group of participants) to engage directly in the problems facing the Congress, and thereby to find out more about Europe at the time. As every pupil is a member of a small team and may be given a particular personality or function within the team it is relatively easy to secure personal involvement, and the extent to which this has occurred can be measured not only during the game itself, but in the course of a term when nineteenth-century European history is studied further.

2. To give all pupils an extended experience in committee work. Through playing the Congress they are very likely to come up against the dangers of being too ambitious, too aggressive, too open to discussion, too subtle or double-faced, and so on. It would be unusual and rather remarkable if classes felt, after the game, that they had in any profound sense 're-enacted' the Congress or had achieved a genuine empathy with those who drew up the original settlement. Such claims can be made far too readily.

## Context

The game is used to introduce fourth-year secondary-school pupils to nineteenth-century European history. In the school where it was devised pupils had had only a little contact with European history up to this point. They had done a second year project on the expansion of Europe in the fifteenth and sixteenth centuries, and had some knowledge of Russian history and of the history of the USA.

## Equipment

The equipment consists of information sheets and outline maps. Each pupil is given

1. Background information (geographical, economic, political, religious) about France, the Empire and Austria, Prussia, Russia, Great Britain and Italy.

2. Background notes on the French Revolutionary and Napoleonic Wars.

3. Notes on the changes Napoleon I made in Europe.

4. Brief biographies, up to 1815, of Castlereagh, Metternich, Alexander I, Hardenberg and Talleyrand.

5. A brief note on the diplomatic world of 1815.

6. Maps of Europe – physical and political in 1715, 1763, 1792, 1810, and a blank outline for use in the Congress.

7. Open-ended questions suggesting lines of thinking.

2, 3, 5, 6 and 7 are reproduced below, together with samples of 1 and 4.

## Operating procedures

A class of, say, thirty is divided into groups of seven to represent Great Britain, Austria, Prussia and Russia, with two acting as observers for France. Each delegation appoints a leader who is responsible for the organization of his delegation and for its activities during Congress.

The teacher introduces the game with a brief talk about the main features of Europe and about the origins and development of the French Revolution and the ensuing European war. Thereafter, the role of the teacher is a passive one. He will supply or discover extra information that the delegation or full congress might need in his role as congress secretary. Otherwise organization rests with the class.

The game usually takes two to three weeks (three forty-minute periods, plus homework, each week) to play. Time is divided, according to the needs of different classes, into plan preparation, full sessions and individual country to country negotiation. Delegations have been most successful where individuals have become specialists in particular areas or in the likely aims of

other countries; success also has related to making contact and
provisional agreements with other countries.

In full session, a chairman, usually from Austria, has been
elected to be responsible for the running of the meeting (Congress). This is a difficult job as sessions tend to become quite
heated and dominant personalities emerge. France is usually
allowed to speak but not to vote, and the Talleyrand figure quite
frequently becomes an important influence on proceedings. An
adaptable agenda is usually drawn up to make decision-making
easier.

A minority of Congresses so far held have produced a full
settlement. On two occasions, war broke out again – once between Prussia and Russia, and once between Prussia and Austria.
In all cases, however, many features of the proposed settlement
were very similar to those in the original settlement.

After the game each pupil writes a report and justification of
the Congress from the point of view of his country. This is
followed by a lesson on the actual settlement and a discussion of
this in relation to the game.

Some samples of the game materials given to pupils:

## 1 Background information: France

*Geography and economy*

The largest country of Western Europe, with mountains in the south and centre, rocky peninsulas and good flat arable land. Climate warmer than Britain with temperate winters.

*Population*

1800 twenty-seven millions. Much the biggest population of any European country. The whole of German-speaking Europe had only twenty-five millions.

All French speaking. By far the most homogeneous state in Europe.

*Agriculture*

On the whole old-fashioned by English standards.

The north-eastern one-third operated medieval open field system, each village having three fields, and three crop rotation.

Some enclosures but even enclosed land managed like unenclosed land.

Southern two-thirds more varied but usually with two crop rotation.

Major agricultural crop grain.

Commercial vineyards.

Surprisingly rare cultivation of potatoes, made for famine if wheat harvest failed.

France could normally supply her own needs in wheat.

*Industry*

France the first to follow Britain's lead into industrialization but development was later and more gradual. For example, in 1815 almost all iron was smelted in charcoal furnaces.

1821, two hundred and twenty-one thousand tons of iron produced.

1807 five million tons of coal produced, almost all in Flanders and Hainault.

Textiles, woollen industry had no factory organization. Peasant production organized by entrepreneurs.

Steam power. Best figures indicate only fifteen establishments were using steam power in 1815, mostly for pumping equipment in mines.

Well-developed urban life with attendant service industries and commercial agricultural.

1801 Paris 548,000
     Marseilles 110,000
     Lyons 109,000
     plus five others over 50,000.

## Trade and communication

Complete network of Roman roads kept up throughout eighteenth century.

Tradition of royal care of roads and canals continued by Napoleon.

Two hundred and twenty-nine separate imperial maintained roads in 1812.

By 1815 France had 1200 kilometres of canals.

Major export wine, sometimes grain and later cotton goods.

Many important ports, but in 1789, only about half imports carried in French ships, major international carriers being Britain and the United States.

Imperial trade largely collapsed after imperial losses at the hands of Britain in the nineteenth century.

By the end of the war France held only Cayenne and various small islands in the Caribbean in the western hemisphere and isolated small areas in Africa and India in the eastern hemisphere.

## Political structure

The *Ancien Régime* came to an end with Louis XVI. Government in eighteenth century France had been theoretically in the hands of an absolute monarch but in practice this was tempered by his ability to control and dominate influential sections of the community, particularly the aristocracy, and some persistently rebellious regions. Throughout the eighteenth century the greatest difficulty for the monarch was shortage of money. The French taxation system was shot through with loopholes.

These loopholes particularly benefited the aristocracy, the church, and certain wealthy towns which had bought exemption.

Political life in France was completely thrown into turmoil by the Revolution. By 1815 Napoleon had imposed one code of law for all France, enforced by efficient centrally directed bureaucrats. Methods of army and civil service recruitment had been altered so that careers in both branches were genuinely open to talent and free of aristocratic prerogative. The power and wealth of the church had been brought under state control. The privileges of the aristocracy had been smashed; serfdom had been abolished. A massive redistribution of land had taken place. In this process many peasants had increased their holdings, many bourgeois had bought land and the new

Napoleonic nobility had taken over some of the estates if not the privileges of the old aristocracy. The political system of the *Ancien Régime* had been largely swept away. But no representative institutions had survived either. Most of all Napoleon had unified France into a single nation with a common law and a common allegiance.

### France in 1815

The losses to France in money and manpower, particularly after 1811, had been ruinous. There was acute labour shortage, industry had been seriously dislocated, as much by the sudden cessation of hostilities as over strain. Unemployed soldiers, war veterans, unemployed munitions workers posed serious social problems. The cumulative psychological shock of the Revolution, the Terror, the Napoleonic victories, and final defeat was prodigious.

## 2 Background notes on French Revolutionary and Napoleonic Wars

There was widespread warfare in Europe from 1792 to 1815, broken only by a temporary truce 1801–3. It is most convenient to think of the war in two phases, the wars of the French Revolutionaries and the wars of Napoleon (1792–1801 and 1803–1815). It became a war of unprecedented scale and there were terribly heavy losses, both of manpower and economy.

The French Revolutionary war broke out because of the fears of Austria, Prussia and the Empire about the international aims of the French who seemed bent on destroying monarchy, not only in France but in the whole of Europe through 'liberation'. Britain joined with opponents to France for similar reasons and also in defence of her trading interests.

The war began with combined Austrian and Prussian attacks from the Low Countries which made deep inroads on the French who, under the Girondins, were unprepared for war. With the accession to power of the Jacobins, however, the French became better organized and regained lost ground. By 1793, the French, under Carnot, were beginning to beat back Prussia, Austria and their allies Holland and Spain into the Low Countries.

The Allies organized their efforts in these early years by means of coalitions – aiming at coordinated effort, largely financed by Britain. These coalitions were difficult to keep together, and their tendency to disintegrate hampered their efforts.

1796 saw the emergence of the young genius of Napoleon as an army commander with his conquest (liberation) of Italy.

### 1796–7 The Italian Campaign

(a) Part of a French three-pronged attack on Austria. Napoleon reorganized dreadful army.

(b) Great victories at Lodi and Rivoli, after which the Austrians surrendered.

(c) Treaty of Campo Formio
    Austria loses Austrian Netherlands
    France sets up and controls Cisalpine Republic
    Austria given the Republic of Venice in recompense.

Napoleon then moved on to capture Egypt as part of a grandiose scheme which included the conquest of India.

### 1798–9 Egyptian Campaign

(a)   Wanted to take Egypt to ruin British trade.
(b)   Captured Malta from the Knights of St John who ruled it.
(c)   July 1798 to Alexandria — massacred the Mamelukes at battle of the Pyramids.
(d)   Nelson destroyed French fleet at the battle of Aboukir Bay.
(e)   Napoleon cut off; conquered Syria as far as Acre; stopped by Sir Sydney Smith. Retreated.
(f)   1799 Made First Consul in new Consulate government in France.

   While Napoleon was in Italy, the Allies had regained much ground in Italy.

### 1800 Second Italian Campaign

(a)   Napoleon recaptures Italy through battle of Marengo.
(b)   French General Moreau defeated Austrians at battle of Hohen-linden.
(c)   1801 Treaty of Luneville
      Austria again recognized French republics in Italy, Switzerland and Holland.
(d)   1802 Treaty of Amiens
      France keeps Belgium
      Britain returns all colonial conquests (see Br. sheet) except Ceylon and Trinidad
      Britain to return Malta to Kts. of St John in three months (Britain had taken from French)
      France to leave Rome and S. Italy and give back Egypt.

   This just a truce. Terms not kept.

### 1803–5 plan to invade England

If Napoleon could invade England, conquest would be easy because the English land forces were feeble. Having conquered England control of the rest of Europe would be easier.

(a)   Napoleon to Boulogne. Tries to control Channel for forty-eight hours.
(b)   British defend south coast. Cornwallis and Nelson on watch.
(c)   Villeneuve (French Admiral) eventually escapes from Toulon with fleet. Villeneuve hops down to Cadiz by August 1805. Napoleon gives up and turns to central Europe.
(d)   October 1805 Villeneuve out again, met and beaten by Nelson at Trafalgar. Britain henceforth dominates sea.

*1805–7 years of triumph for Napoleon*

Napoleon now conquered mainland Europe in a series of remarkable victories which confirmed his position as the leading general of his age and one of the outstanding military geniuses of all time.

(a)  1805 Battle of Ulm. Napoleon smashes Austria and occupies Vienna.

Battle of Austerlitz. Napoleon smashes Austria and Russia.

(b)  1806 Peace of Pressberg
Austria surrenders for third time
Austria gives up Venice, Tyrol ; Holy Roman Empire goes.

(c)  1806 Battle of Jena ; Prussia crushed.

(d)  1807 Battle of Friedland ; Russia defeated, Alexander capitulates.
Treaty of Tilsit
France makes peace with Prussia and Russia
Russia joins Continental System (see below).

Having conquered Europe, Napoleon forced the major powers into humiliating alliance with France. Most importantly, they were forced by the Berlin and Milan Decrees to join in an economic blockade of Europe directed against Britain. All European ports would thus be closed to Britain who would, it was hoped, thus be starved into submission. Britain replied with similar blockade aimed at preventing European trade. Neither embargo succeeded in its aim, but the Continental System of Napoleon was expensive and difficult to maintain. (Look at the length of the European coastline.) It was also increasingly annoying to France's 'allies', notably Russia.

*1807–13 The Peninsular War*

A revolt in Spain (2 May 1808) against the new ruler, Joseph Napoleon, and unrest in Portugal, allowed the British to get a foothold in Europe. The war, in which Britain hoped eventually to invade France by way of the westerly gap in the Pyrenees, was for five years a stalemate. This was more injurious to France than to Britain. The French were in unfriendly territory and forced to camp in the cold Spanish plain during the winters, whereas the British under Wellesley (Wellington) were well quartered and had the support of the native population.

(a)  1809 Wellesley takes over from Sir John Moore and clears Portugal of French.

(b)  1809 Wellesley builds defence lines of Torres Vedras behind which British were quartered in winter.

(c) 1810 Massena (French) with 350,000 in all-out attack. Suffers in winter.

(d) 1810–12 Wellesley tries to take Spanish forts of Badajoz and Ciudad Roderigo.

(e) 1812 Napoleon withdraws troops from Spain for attack on Russia. Wellesley takes Madrid, but withdraws for winter to Ciudad Roderigo.

(f) 1813 Wellesley across Spain to foot of Pyrenees.

(g) 1814 Wellesley enters France and part of War of Liberation of Fourth Coalition.

## 1812–15 The decline and fall of Napoleon

Tsar Alexander I became disenchanted with alliance with Napoleon, in particular with the Continental System. Napoleon therefore attacks Russia to beat into submission (army of 600,000 troops). The Russians adopted tactics of retreat and 'scorched earth' i.e. burning all they left behind them. In this way Napoleon's lines of communication became impossibly stretched.

(a) 1812 Battle of Borodino outside Moscow. Russians set fire to Moscow.

(b) French retreat to avoid Russian winter. Army destroyed by weather and guerrilla attacks.

(c) Fourth Coalition formed (Britain, Russia, Austria, Prussia). Napoleon manages remarkable recovery – puts 250,000 troops into battle but finally beaten at battle of Dresden. Surrenders.

This surrender was followed by initial peace treaties and then by what was to be the final settlement (Peace of Paris). However, Napoleon returned to France and led a national revival for three months (the Hundred Days) of false success. Finally beaten at battle of Waterloo by combined leadership of Wellington and Blucher.

## 3 How Napoleon changed Europe

When Napoleon had conquered or suppressed Europe he redrew traditional divisions to suit his purposes. Thus Europe became his and France's Empire — the biggest European Empire since Roman times. However it lasted only eight years. Supplement this outline by reference to the maps of Europe in 1793 and 1810.

*French Empire ruled directly by Napoleon*

The French Republic had already acquired :
The Netherlands
the left bank of the Rhine
Savoy and Piedmont
Napoleon added :
the whole of N W Italy, including Rome
the Illyrian Provinces, with ports of Trieste and Fiume
Holland, giving him control of its important commerce (until 1810 a dependent state ruled by his brother Louis)
N W Germany, including the port of Hamburg.

*Dependent States ruled indirectly by Napoleon*

Switzerland (Napoleon was President of the Helvetic Republic.)
Kingdom of Italy (Napoleon was king; his stepson, Eugene, was Viceroy.)
Kingdom of Naples (Napoleon's brother-in-law, Murat, was King.)
Confederation of the Rhine (Most of Germany, except Prussia and Austria, was united in this Confederation, Napoleon being President.)
Kingdom of Westphalia included in Confederation of the Rhine (Napoleon's brother, Jerome, was King.)
Grand Duchy of Warsaw (Union of Prussian and Austrian parts of former Poland entrusted to Napoleon's ally, the King of Saxony.)
Kingdom of Spain (Napoleon's brother, Joseph, was installed in 1808.)

Because most of these areas were ruled by members of Napoleon's family, they were in effect ruled by Napoleon himself. Forced to supply troops and money and to accept his code of law. Italy was more leniently treated than the German parts.

*Compulsory allies*

Prussia : After Jena, in 1806, Prussia forced to submit to Napoleon, though she used the enforced peace to reorganize herself under ministers such as Stein, Scharnhorst, Gneisenau and Hardenberg.

Austria : Austria rebelled against Napoleon after the Peace of Pressberg (1806) but was defeated a fourth time at Wagram (1809) and forced into unwilling alliance for four years.

Denmark including Norway.

Thus, in 1810, all Europe except Russia (a free ally), the Ottoman Empire, Portugal and Great Britain, was under the influence of Napoleon.

## 4 Talleyrand 1754-1838 : biographical notes

French diplomatist and statesman who began his career in the church. From Reims, where he was sub-deacon, he moved to Paris in 1778, and was appointed Bishop of Autun in 1789. He sided with the revolutionaries in the States-General, and proposed the confiscation of church lands ! Resigned his see in 1791, and was put under the ban of the church by the Pope.

In the same year he entered the field of diplomacy, and was sent to London in 1792 as a Diplomatic Representative. Convinced that England would not go to war against France unless the Netherlands were attacked, he also declared the Declaration of Pillnitz a 'loud-sounding nothing'. Then France declared war, Talleyrand was expelled from Britain and went to the United States.

On the establishment of the Directory he returned to France and was made Foreign Minister. Sensing the collapse of the Directory in 1799, he resigned and then assisted Napoleon in his Brumaire coup d'etat. The reward for this foresight and help was that he was given the same office (Foreign Minister) under the new regime.

Under Napoleon, Talleyrand worked hard to improve his country's interests, perpetually urging moderation on Napoleon. He was not very successful in this, largely because he didn't have a free hand. Although he could not prevent Napoleon from crushing Austria in 1805, he did play an important part in the establishment of the Confederation of the Rhine. After Tilsit, Talleyrand, feeling that Napoleon was over-reaching himself, resigned. Though he was retained in Napoleon's Council, Talleyrand now played a double game by secretly corresponding with the Tsar warning him that Napoleon intended to use Russia's influence at the Erfurt Conference (1808) to keep Austria out of the war. During these years he grew increasingly mistrustful of Napoleon. At the beginning of the Moscow campaign he said, 'It is the beginning of the end.'

Resigned from the Council early 1814. On the surrender of Paris to the allies, Talleyrand convened the Senate (sixty-four out of the one hundred and forty attended) and they pronounced Napoleon to have forfeited the crown. Talleyrand was sent as French observer to Vienna and expediently stayed there during the period of the Hundred Days

## 5 Note on diplomatic world and background to congress

The diplomatic world was small. As Europe was largely composed of autocratic states dominated by kings, princes and aristocracy, such people constituted the diplomatic class. Many knew each other well. and men of this class certainly would have more in common with each other than with members of the lower orders in their own countries. This sense of oneness was reinforced by the fact that all diplomats spoke French which had become the *lingua franca* of Europe, replacing Latin. Kings were primarily responsible for the foreign policies of their dominions and, however powerful an individual minister might be, he had to defer to his monarch. The main exception to this general situation was Britain, where ministers were as responsible to Parliament as to the King.

The Congress provided an opportunity for a gigantic festival for Europe's aristocrats. Napoleon, and the ideas of the French Revolution, seemed to have been finally beaten and the ruling classes could set about enjoying themselves as of old. The host, Emperor Francis I, was extremely generous and Vienna was an ideal setting for the Congress. An old and beautiful city, it was a great centre of culture and the arts. Mozart and Haydn had only recently died and Beethoven was still composing. During the months of the Congress concerts, plays and state balls followed each other in a seemingly unending stream.

The main representatives at the Congress were:

1. Guests of the Emperor: Frederick I of Wurtemberg, Elector William of Hesse, Grand-Duke George of Hesse-Darmstadt, Maximilian Joseph of Bavaria, Frederick VI of Denmark, Karl August Duke of Weimar.

2. For Prussia: The King, Prince Hardenberg (chief spokesman), assisted by Humboldt and group of experts, including statistician Hoffmann.

3. For Russia: Alexander I, Razumovski, Nesselrode (foreign minister of German extraction), Stein (exiled Prussian reformer), Czartoryski (Polish), Pozo di Borgo (Corsican enemy of Napoleon). Alexander dominated.

4. For France: Talleyrand, Duc de Dalberg, Comte de la Besdenardiers and staff.

5. For Britain: Castlereagh (chief), Stewart (Castlereagh's half-brother, eccentric and foolish), Cathcart (friend of Alexander and Ambassador to Russia), Clancarty (principal assistant) and officials to avoid Austrian spy system.

**6. For Austria:** Metternich (chief), von Messenberg and assistants and experts especially von Gentz, who was secretary to Metternich and unofficial secretary to Congress.

Despite the many minor rulers who attended, the Congress was effectively in the hands of Austria, Prussia, Russia and Britain with France keeping a close but only semi-official eye on proceedings.

Europe – structure and relief

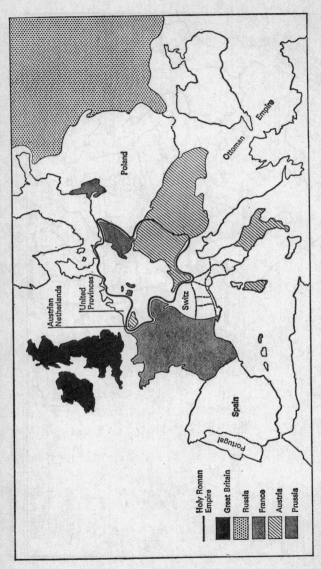

Europe in 1715

Holy Roman Empire
Great Britain
Russia
France
Austria
Prussia

Poland

Ottoman Empire

Austrian Netherlands

United Provinces

Switz.

Spain

Portugal

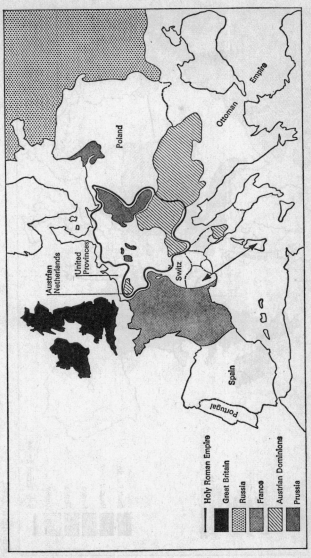

Europe in 1763

Holy Roman Empire
Great Britain
Russia
France
Austrian Dominions
Prussia

Poland

Ottoman Empire

Austrian Netherlands
United Provinces
Switz

Spain

Portugal

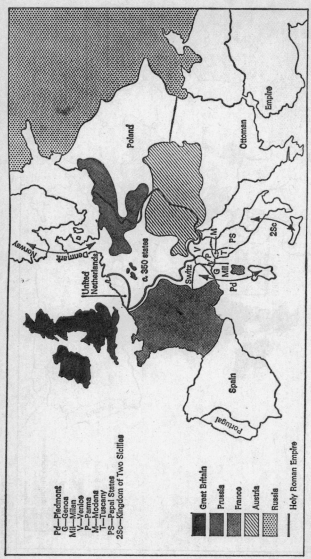

Europe in 1792

Pd—Piedmont
G—Genoa
Mil—Milan
V—Venice
P—Parma
M—Modena
T—Tuscany
PS—Papal States
2Sc—Kingdom of Two Sicilies

Great Britain
Prussia
France
Austria
Russia

Holy Roman Empire

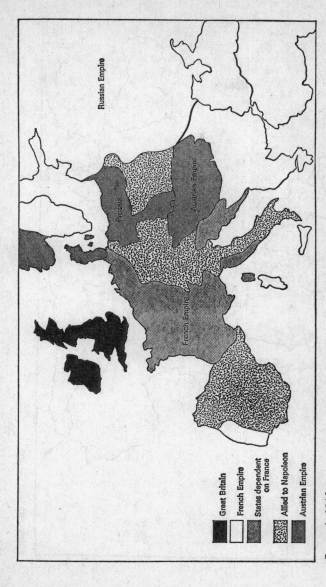

Europe in 1810

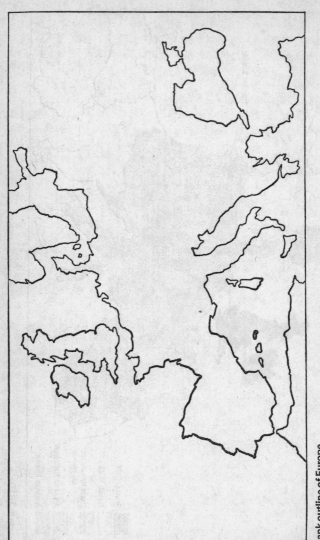

Blank outline of Europe

## 7 Suggested lines of thinking

1. What sort of Europe would you want?

2. What would happen to France? How heavily would she be punished? Would you prescribe a form of government? If so, what? Would France be brought back as a great power?

3. Would your country want territorial gains? If so what?

4. Would you want security safeguards? If so what?

5. Would you want to prevent any other powers making certain gains?

6. What would you do about the smaller states? Before the French Revolution there were:
   The United Netherlands
   c. 360 states in the Holy Roman Empire (biggest were Prussia Bavaria, Saxony, Hanover)
   Switzerland
   Kingdom of Sardinia; Genoa; Milan; Parma; Modena; Tuscany; Lucca; Republic of Venice; Papal States; Kingdom of Two Sicilies; Poland; Denmark and Norway; Sweden.

7. How would you ensure future peace? (If you wanted it.)

8. Would you want a final peace now, or use this for future manoeuvre?

We hope that your Congress will produce a full final treaty, but should it break down it will be your duty to explain in your final report exactly why it broke down and what the immediate consequences of the breakdown were. This should be detailed. However, your aim is to produce a Treaty, and you will have failed badly if you fail in this.

# Chapter 11
# The Conservation Game

Devised by David Lewis and S. McB. Carson for
Hertfordshire Education Committee

## Aims

The game aims to present the complexity of considerations in
siting a new airport and its accessories, illustrating the environmental conflicts between the basic locational needs in a least-
cost analysis and the pressures for conservation. Cases are
presented from both sides in the search for an acceptable com-
promise site. Besides the airport itself, urban centres, new communications and public services have to be located and routed.

## Context

The activities of the Roskill Commission and of European Conservation Year initially presented the opportunity to develop the
game. It was used on several occasions in individual schools, and
at specially arranged day conferences, when groups of fifth and
sixth formers from different schools came together to play the
game. On these latter occasions, participants were provided with
briefs for study before the day of the game, and the session was
sometimes prefaced by a talk from a local planning officer. Assessment by outside 'experts' was made on the final presentations of
groups. The game lasts profitably for three to six hours.

Pupils are asked to put themselves in the position of those
concerned about the site of a third London airport. Whereas the
final deliberations of the Roskill Commission were confined to a
choice of four sites, this simulation offers unlimited opportunities
for comparing the merits of any number of sites.

## Equipment

Each group is given:

1. A map of the counties sixty miles north and east of London
(scale 1:100,000) on which have also been marked the following:

(a) Built-up areas (emphasized).
(b) Agricultural land quality (in three major categories). Information derived from 1:625,000 O S Land Classification Map.
(c) Areas of high landscape value. Information derived from Planning Officers of County Councils in the area.
(d) Conservation areas. Information derived as in (c).
(e) Sites of Special Scientific Interest and National Nature Reserves. Information derived from published lists supplied by the Nature Conservancy.

A unit of one square kilometre is the smallest basic unit handled in the game, and areas are 'squared off' to this shape.

2. Two acetate transparencies with an airport site marked. Information derived from the Wilson Committee Report on Noise, and other publications.

One transparency was at scale 1:100,000 for work on the base map and showed 45 and 55 N N I contours. But the 1:100,000 map does not show relief. A second transparency of the airport area only at scale 1:63,630 was therefore provided for use with 1″ O S maps.

3. Sheets giving details of costs and details of conservation points.

4. Blank sheets to be used when costing projects.

5. A role-brief for each individual in the group, together with supporting literature and maps as appropriate.

1:63,360 O S maps were available for consultation by 'airport engineers', for the assessment of the variation of height over any proposed site.

The area covered by such maps was that of O S one-inch maps 134–7, 146–50, 159–62.

## Operating procedures

Groups of between fifteen and twenty students can operate as one 'commission', with a teacher acting as Chairman if required. With a group of fifteen, roles can be allocated as follows:

2   Panel of assessors and accountants

Civil engineers – consultants to the responsible bodies as indicated:

2   airport site
1   town site
1   communications

Public services engineers – planners to the responsible bodies as indicated:

2   water
2   electricity
2   sewage

Conservationists:

1   representing the interests of farmers (National Farmers' Union)
1   representing the interests of country landowners
2   representing the interests of Naturalists' Trusts and Associations
2   representing the interests of amenity bodies (Ramblers' Association, Council for the Preservation of Rural England, Noise Abatement Society)
1   representing the interests of historians and archaeologists

The Chairman distributes role-briefs accordingly, preferably in advance so that there may be preliminary reading.

Groups are told that the object of the game is to site an airport on the map as economically as possible and with the minimum loss of conservation points. In addition there must be provided:

(a) A town (or a number of towns or extensions of existing towns) totalling fifty square kilometres in area, with satisfactory road links to the airport.
(b) Motorway connections to the London Ring Road system shown on the map.
(c) Railway connections to London.
(d) Provision for both town and airport in respect of water, electricity and sewage disposal facilities.

(As the game is played in units of one square kilometre, if a route passes diagonally through a square kilometre or if the airport site includes any part of a square it is counted as completely occupying that square.)

Costs are incurred and conservation points lost for any square occupied as shown on the respective sheets.

When each player is familiar with his briefing documents, discussion begins. Engineers confer and present a case for a site (or more than one site) to the Chairman and the assessors in the group. Conservationists watch the activities of the engineers and must be kept advised of likely choices in order to consider the possible conservation effects.

Once a possible site is identified, communications engineers prepare and cost routes; town site engineers suggest urban areas and agree communications and public services; public-services engineers prepare routes for electricity supply, water supply and the disposal of sewage.

The Chairman allows the ordered presentation of cases and the replies to them. Assessors check cost sheets and conservation point sheets for accuracy.

Eventually, there may be agreement by all on the 'best' site; alternatively the Chairman and assessors may come to a majority verdict amongst themselves.

A member of the team then presents the final site on the map with cost and conservation points noted. If more than one group is working at the same time there can then be the presentation of each *group's* chosen site, and an assessment of these by an overall Board of Chairmen and assessors or by a planning and conservation officer invited to evaluate the arguments.

Costs used in the game are as real as can be ascertained; but the assessment of conservation points is necessarily more subjective.

Some groups may choose to rate the need to save 'conservation points' as a relatively low priority; others may see this as an important issue, and make their airports and facilities much more expensive as a result. The incompatibility of the two scales is no bar to a consideration of the relative importance of least-cost analysis and conservation values – quite the reverse.

Some samples of the game materials given to pupils:

## General advice to participants

The *purpose* of the game is to present cases.

The *object* of the game is to site a new airport and supporting town with rail and road connections, electricity, water and sewage provision with due regard to conservation requirements, which have been classified into four main groups:

1. National Nature Reserves protected by law against development and managed by the Nature Conservancy.

2. Sites of Special Scientific Interest i.e. areas designated by the Nature Conservancy as being of special interest and requiring consultation between planning authorities and the Nature Conservancy in the event of development proposal.

3. Conservation Areas, usually designated by local Authorities.

4. Areas of high landscape value, usually designated by local authority planners.

You have been allocated a role to play. Essential data is provided but obviously in the time allowed it would be impossible to provide all the information on any site – nor would you have time to absorb it.

Please use your imagination too. Although the data is as realistic as possible you may add your own arguments and even invent local details to add realism if you wish (or to demolish other people's arguments!).

It will help a great deal if you can give some thought to the part you are to play before coming to the game itself. There are many books on these controversial subjects that will help you. Have a browse through your library.

Please see that you can read and use the Grid Reference System (S S S Is are listed using six-figure references but four-figure references are all that are required.)

It is not intended that the game should be concerned in any way with sites being considered by the Roskill commission.

## General table of costs for reference
*Buying land for airport, towns, railways, roads*

| | | |
|---|---|---|
| Red | £1,250,000 per square kilometre | |
| Blue | £ 125,000 | " |
| White | £ 75,000 | " |
| Yellow | £ 50,000 | " |

### Construction of Airport

| | |
|---|---|
| On land | £400,000,000 total |
| On tidal areas or sea | £800,000,000 |

Additional levelling costs. For each 50 ft. variation over the site £50,000,000.

### Construction of town on 50 square kilometres

Initial capital outlay £200,000,000
Excess charge for building upwards.
For each square kilometre *less* than 50, £5000 to be charged on *each* remaining square.
Provision of link roads to airport £500,000 per kilometre.

### Construction of motorways and railways

| | |
|---|---|
| Initial costs motorways | £1,000,000 per kilometre |
| New railways | £1,000,000 " |
| Improved railways | £ 500,000 ' |
| Excess charge beyond 30 kilometres from Tower Bridge | £1,000,000 " |

### Construction of electricity pylons

| | |
|---|---|
| Construction of line terminal stations at each end of each line and wherever lines | £25,000 per kilometre |
| branch | £10,000 each |

### Construction of water supply lines

| | |
|---|---|
| Construction of pipe-line | £100,000 per kilometre |
| Excess charge for passing through built-up area | £ 50,000 " |
| Purification plants | £ 50,000 each |

### Construction of sewage disposal

| | |
|---|---|
| Construction of pipe-line | £100,000 per kilometre |
| Excess charge for passing through built-up area | £ 50,000 " |
| Sewage purification plants | £ 50,000 each |

*Compensation and compulsory purchase rates*

*Compulsory purchase*

Clearance of all built-up land within the
55-decibel area
Demolition of all built-up areas within
5 kilometres of runway ends

} £1,250,000
per square
kilometre

*Compensation to farmers*

Within the 45-decibel area or crossed by
roads or railways  £1000 per square kilometre
For land crossed by pylons, water pipes
or sewage pipes  £100 per square kilometre
For farms destroyed in airport and town site
  £25,000 per square kilometre

# General table of conservation points, for reference

*Loss of land*

| | Points per square kilometre |
|---|---|

Loss of agricultural land (blue, white or yellow squares) in construction of airport, town, motorways, railways and included in 55-decibel area    2

Inclusion of agricultural land in 45-decibel area    2

Inclusion of built-up land (red squares) in 45-decibel area    10

If crossed by pylons    10

*Areas of high landscape value*

If included in 55-decibel area    30

If used in construction area (airport, town, road, railway)    20

If included in 45-decibel area

    built-up land (red)    10

    agricultural land (blue, white yellow)    2

(charged *in addition* to items above)

If crossed by pylons    20

*National Nature Reserve (red dot with N)*

If used in any construction area (airport, town, road, railway)    1000

*S S S I s (red dots)*

If used in any construction area (airport, town, road, railway) or in 55-decibel area of 5 km from either ends of runways    40

If included in 55-decibel area on built-up land or agricultural land double the charges in item above i.e. 20 or 4

*Conservation areas (blue dots)*

If used in any construction area (airport, town, road, railway) or included in 55-decibel area or 5 km from either end of runway    40

If included in 45-decibel area or built up land or agricultural land double the charges in item above i.e. 20 or 4

If crossed by pylons          10

Note : If the conservation area or S S S I is in an
    area of high landscape value the points for both
    charges are added together.

Sewage disposal and river pollution
    For each 1 million gallon per day above the
    minimum permissible discharge at the point
    of entry to the river system        10

# Airport engineers: costing sheet
*Cost of buying land in square kilometres*

*For each square used, put a stroke in this column e.g. 4 squares ////
Each 5th square is shown *HHt*

| Colour | Number of squares* | Total | Cost per km² | Cost |
|--------|--------------------|-------|--------------|------|
| Red    |                    |       |              |      |
| Blue   |                    |       |              |      |
| White  |                    |       |              |      |
| Yellow |                    |       |              |      |
| Initial cost of construction |    |       |              |      |
| Cost of levelling land       |    |       |              |      |
|        |                    |       | Total cost   |      |

## Brief: Civil Engineers (Airport) responsible to the British Airports Authorities

1. The Airport will cost £400,000,000 to build.

2. The site must take into account existing inbound and outbound routes of Heathrow and Gatwick. For this purpose see attached map (not included here. A map with this information is included in the Report of the Roskill Commission (HMSO) — Eds.).

3. No extra charge is incurred if the site is thirty kilometres from Tower Bridge or less. For every additional kilometre measured to the centre of the airport site an additional £1,000,000 to cover extra operating costs will be incurred, this will be accounted for by the Communications Engineers.

4. You must work closely with the Civil Engineer — Communications whose responsibility it is to build a motorway from the airport to connect it to the London Ring Road and a railway to connect it to the rail system.

5. You must discuss with the Civil Engineer (Towns) the siting of his town of 50 square kilometres and the linkage of this to the airport by good road services.

6. The airport must be level. For every 50 ft variation in the height from highest to lowest point on the site the cost will be an additional £50,000,000. Check the 1 :63,360 Contour map.

7. Watch the drainage and other features of relief. (You cannot build an airport over a major river system.)

8. Ensure the minimum loss of conservation points. Every conservation area, SSSI or square kilometre of land of high landscape value will be charged (see scale). However, these will be charged by the conservationists, you are not concerned with counting them.

9. Any built-up area five kilometres away from the ends of the runways will have to be bought for demolition of existing houses.

10. *Purchase of land*

Four categories. Land must be bought at the following rates:

Red  Built-up areas.
   Cost £1,250,000 per square kilometre.
Blue  Exceptionally good agricultural land.
   Cost £125,000 per square kilometre.
White  Good quality agricultural land.
   Cost £75,000 per square kilometre.
Yellow Second quality agricultural land.
   Cost £50,000 per square kilometre.

## 11. *Criteria*

Consider these points very carefully and keep a watching brief in case you need to adjust your site.

Any selected site — whatever its other attributes — must, of course, be operationally satisfactory for the air traffic which it is designed to serve. Under the terms of the Airports Authority Act the Authority has to pay its way. Therefore the new airport must also be economically satisfactory. The airport must be so situated that it can fulfil its purpose of being readily accessible to the growing volume of passenger and cargo traffic from London and its environs.

The essential requirements of a major international airport, and the question of minimizing disturbance to the surrounding locality, clearly present a most difficult area for judgement between operational, national, local and the wider social interests — that is between the broad purposes to be served, the interests to be satisfied, and specifications to be achieved and the requirements to be met.

## 12. *The basic requirements*

There are seven basic requirements against which the merits of all the alternative sites for a Third London Airport must be judged. They are:

### (a) *Operational suitability*

Including the terrain, weather, Air Traffic Control, compatibility with other airports and suitability for safe and economic operations. On present evidence, preferably in a sector from North of London, on grounds of Air Traffic Control, of traffic 'catchment area' and of compatibility with Heathrow and Gatwick.

### (b) *Area for development*

For a four-runway airport with adequate space for runways of the required lengths and for the necessary separation between the runways, it is essential to have available an area of level land of not less than about 8000 acres, preferably inclined on a north-east/south-west heading because of the prevailing wind. (The transparency provided shows this size to scale and orientation.)

### (c) *Acceptability to airlines*

An airport must be commercially satisfactory to airlines in a competitive situation. A new airport to serve London's air traffic must satisfy the airlines' commercial requirements for the provision of services which will be competitive with those of other London airports — in total journey times and costs. It must be satisfactory to airlines in comparison with competitive airports across the Channel.

### (d) *Accessibility*

An airport must be within reasonable distance of the centres of population to be served, and of available road and rail systems. As close in time and distance — (and hence reasonable in cost) — as can be achieved to the centre of London. It may not be possible to persuade airlines to accept a move to a relatively remote site (which might have serious competitive disadvantages in journey costs and time) when their competitors are still able to operate services through more accessible airports.

There would be a permanent advantage to the community — in time and money — if the new airport is built on a site which is easily accessible for passengers, cargo and the staff working at the airport.

The best operational layout will be of no use — and inconsistent with the Authority's duties and purpose — unless it is viable and is in a location where the airlines and the travelling public will use it. In short — no amount of financial subsidy will prevent a 'London Airport' too far from London being a white elephant.

### (e)  Economic viability

The capital and running costs chargeable to the Authority must be compatible with the Airport paying its way at charges which users can reasonably be expected to pay. It must be sited so that an airport can be constructed in stages and operated at an economic cost — including terminals, taxiways, access roads and other amenities — and hence be capable of paying its way.

### (f)  Community interests

The site must be such that the airport can be integrated satisfactorily with the prospective future social and economic patterns of the area, and located to take full account of the effects on the neighbouring population, on land use, nature conservation, buildings and other objects of historic and social importance, as well as taking account of the growth of population and employment opportunities.

In essence, therefore, it is believed that a site for a new major airport would be acceptable to all the many interests concerned were it possible to reconcile the conflicting aspects.

Satisfactory to operate (safe and suitable)
Convenient for the air traveller (near and accessible)
Compatible with amenities (secluded and quiet)
Attractive for employment (busy and diverse)
Economic to the airlines (accessible and large)
Viable to the owner (economic and efficient)

No location ideally meets all the requirements.

### 13. Coastal and inland sites

In some countries coastal sites have been selected for major airports. All of them possess the great advantage of a close proximity to the cities which they serve. In the United Kingdom some, more distant, coastal sites may be found, where the impact of noise on local communities would be less than at some inland sites — although such inland sites might be preferred on other grounds. Account must be taken of the fact that construction costs would be substantially higher on most of the coastal sites which have been proposed than at a number of possible inland sites. Too heavy a construction cost would impose upon the Authority a crippling burden of debt or on the air transport industry an unreasonable level of charges. The cost in this case must be taken as double the construction costs given in paragraph 1, e.g. £800,000,000.

14. *Compensation claims* will be made for land compulsorily purchased but this will be done by the National Farmers' Union representative and you need not account for this.

## Brief for Representatives of Nature Conservancy and Naturalists' Trusts

1. You represent the Nature Conservancy, a department of the Government, and Naturalists' Trusts, which are voluntary bodies keen to conserve the natural history of their country.

2. You have the responsibility of opposing the loss of any of the Sites of Special Scientific Interest that may be involved in any siting or routing of communications. Sites marked N are National Nature Reserves and may not be disturbed without the authority of an Act of Parliament. Other sites are marked w th a red circle. The details of each are given in the list of SSSIs drawn up by the Nature Conservancy.

3. You can also make a more general case for the loss of open country which is a wildlife habitat (woodland, hedges or streams in particular).

4. You will obviously not have all the facts about any SSSI or area of the country and you are allowed (indeed encouraged) to exercise your magination a little in order to put your case.

5. It will help if you can give some thought beforehand to the need for the conservation of species of plants and animals that are in danger of extinction in the south-east of England. The library is likely to contain many books on the natural history of the region.

6. Conservation Points are charged for areas that would be destroyed by the airport site, town site or by any road or railway.
   Loss of an SSSI – 40 points

7. The Farmers' representatives will argue the case for financial compensation for the loss of agricultural land but you must claim conservation points for any agricultural land lost to represent the wild life habitats in hedges, woodland, streams or fields, at two points per square.

8. Inclusion of such areas in the noise contours will be dealt with by the representatives of the Noise Abatement Society.

9. You must vigorously argue the case for any SSSI but note that the inclusion of any National Nature reserve (N) would involve an Act of Parliament and is charged one thousand points.

10. Check on the rivers being used for sewage disposal (Public Services Engineers).

The Royal Commission on Sewage Disposal required that the treated effluent must be discharged where it totalled not more than one eighth of the river flow. To allow for the other effluent already in the river this figure must be revised to one-tenth.

11. Maps are provided showing the minimum river flows in millions of gallons per day for rivers in the region.

The effluent from the town sites will be at an average rate of forty gallons per person per day. (Ten million gallons per day.) The airport effluent can be regarded as five million gallons per day. Where the effluent is discharged into a river at a higher rate than one tenth of the water flow, conservation points are incurred at ten points for every million gallons per day involved.

Check that if treated effluents are taken direct to the sea, the pipes are led twenty km beyond the coastline.

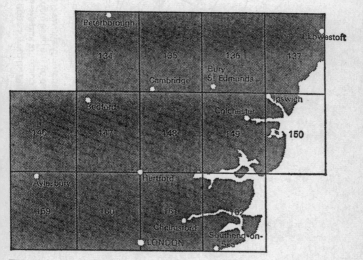

This diagram represents the area covered by the map used in the game. The numbers refer to the 1″ O S maps which cover the area

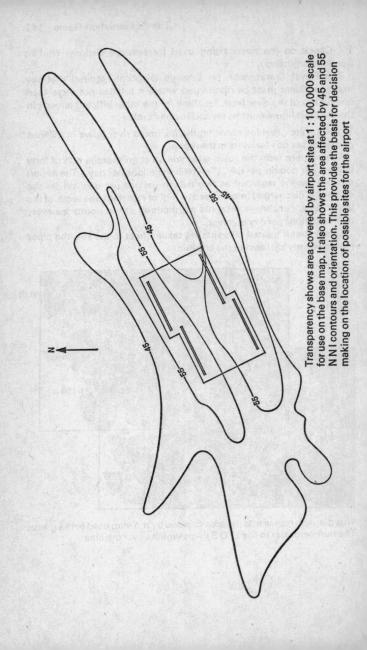

Transparency shows area covered by airport site at 1 : 100,000 scale for use on the base map. It also shows the area affected by 45 and 55 N N I contours and orientation. This provides the basis for decision making on the location of possible sites for the airport

N

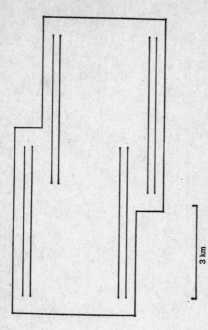

3 km

Transparency shows area covered by airport site at 1 : 63,360 scale
for checking height variation of proposed sites on 1" O S maps.
See note 2 under Equipment

# Part Three
## Sources of Material for the Classroom

There have already been several classifications and directories of
game and simulation material issued, and these are noted for
further reference below. This further addition cannot claim
complete comprehensiveness in its field since much material is
difficult to trace and keep up to date. It differs slightly from some
of its companion directories, however, in attempting to list
*published* game and simulation material designed specifically for
educational use.

The directory does *not* include commercial games, produced
primarily for entertainment purposes which may nevertheless be
considered to have some useful simulation properties worth using
in the classroom (e.g. Diplomacy, Pit, Risk, Gettysburg, etc.).
The directory also omits a large number of American war and
battle games which have been devised, and which may also in
certain circumstances be used in schools.

A large number of the simulations are of American origin. (A
minority of these are obtainable through English publishing
firms, but most need to be obtained by reference direct to
American addresses.) It is in the U S A that most work has been
done in this field, and inevitably this is reflected in the published
state of the art.

The U S A has spawned such simulation design teams as Abt
Associates, and Project Simile, and particular publishing firms
(such as Western) owe their origins to simulation research.
Groups such as B O C E S and Interact represent semi-commercial
approaches to simulation design and development for educational
purposes.

American curriculum projects have also commissioned and
used a good deal of simulation material. But the vast majority of
innovatory simulation systems seem to stem from enthusiastic
individuals, many of whom have a greater interest in design and
operation than in the marketing of ideas.

The directory attempts to give information about the generally
used title of classroom simulations, and a short description of the

theme of the exercise; it has not been practically possible to include any kind of critique, or indication of current price. The directory also lists the operational requirements of the game in terms of players and time needed, the form which the materials take, and gives some indication of the level at which the simulation is most useful. (In relation to this, the overlapping classification has been developed as follows; A = primary-school level (7–11); B = middle-school level (9–14); C = senior-school level (13–18).)

However, as has already been pointed out, simulations can often be adapted for use at many levels, and this information is presented for initial guidance rather than proscription. It is to be hoped that the astute teacher will adapt and develop material as fits needs and demands.

The designers' and/or suppliers' names and addresses are also added, and may be potential sources for further simulation material. Inclusion of the simulation does not guarantee current availability, however, or necessarily imply a willingness to deal with general inquiries.

Finally, at the end of the listing of selected simulation models, three separate varieties of further information are summarized. These three summaries identify sources of further guidance which may be accessible through available bibliographies, films and series publications.

# Chapter 12
# A Directory of Selected Simulation Material

**C Blue Wodjet Company.** A business simulation concerning the problems of pollution for industry.

*Requirements*
25–30 players
4–6 hours

*Designers/Suppliers*
Interact
P O Box 1023
Lakeside
California
USA

**A+ Bushman Hunting.** An elementary simulation of the primitive social organization of bushman life in the Kalahari Desert.

*Requirements*
5–10 players
1 hour
Mimeographed materials

*Designers/Suppliers*
Educational Development Center
55 Chapel Street
Newton
Massachusetts
USA

**A-B Bus Service.** Groups simulate bus-operators, seeking to build efficient networks of routes on an island.

*Requirements*
6–8 players
30–40 minutes
Printed rules and instructions

*Designers/Suppliers*
In *Games in Geography*,
Rex Walford (1969),
Longman

**A+ Caribou Hunting.** A game which explores the relationship between technology and social organization in the Netsilik Eskimos Community of Pelly Bay. The simulation uses caribou hunting in the community as a focus for both action and discussion.

*Requirements*
3 players
1 hour
Mimeographed materials

*Designers/Suppliers*
Educational Development Center
55 Chapel Street
Newton
Massachusetts
USA

**C+ Clug (Community Land Use Game).** A simulation of urban land-use interactions which has been compared with combinations of chess and Monopoly and is capable of considerable elaboration.

| *Requirements* | *Designers/Suppliers* |
| --- | --- |
| 9 players (min.) | Systems Gaming Associates |
| 3 hours (min.) | Triphammer Road |
| Packaged materials and kit | Ithaca |
| | NY 14850 |
| | USA |

**C Community Disaster.** A simulation of a community hit by a localized natural disaster.

| *Requirements* | *Designers/Suppliers* |
| --- | --- |
| 6–16 players | Western Publishing Co. Inc. |
| 2–6 hours | School and Library Department |
| Packaged materials | 850 Third Avenue |
| | New York |
| | NY 10022 |
| | USA |
| | Also: |
| | 14/16 Great Portland Street |
| | London W1 |

**C Conflict (Preliminary edition).** The simulation is centred on a crisis which erupts in 1999 in a world disarmed by universal agreement and policed by three international councils (based on Waskow's peacekeeping model described in *Keeping the World Disarmed* and published by the Centre for the Study of Democratic Institutions).

| *Requirements* | *Designers/Suppliers* |
| --- | --- |
| 24–36 players | World Law Fund |
| 2–3 hours | 11 West 42nd Street |
| Packaged materials | New York |
| | NY 10036 |
| | USA |

**B Consumer.** A consumer-buying-process simulation involving players in problems stemming from instalment buying.

*Requirements*
11–34 players
1½–2½ hours
Packaged materials

*Designers/Suppliers*
Western Publishing Co. Inc.
School and Library Department
850 Third Avenue
New York
N Y 10022
U S A

Also:
14/16 Great Portland Street
London W1

**B+ Crisis.** A simulation of international conflict in which teams endeavour to manage the affairs of six fictitious nations.

*Requirements*
18–36 players
1–2 hours

Instruction manual plus
consumable forms

*Designers/Suppliers*
Project Simile P O Box 1023
1150 Silverado
La Jolla
California 92037
U S A

**B+C. Crisis in Lagia.** A simulation concerning aspects of war and society in four parts:
Outbreak of war
Morale and attitudes
The concept of a just war
Protest.

*Requirements*
25–30 players
1–2 hours

Mimeographed materials

*Designers/Suppliers*
Humanities Curriculum Project
Centre for Applied Research
in Education
University of East Anglia
University Village
Norwich
N O R 88

**B + Deciding Priorities for Aid.** Two role-playing case studies centred on Botswana and Upper Volta which put the players in a position where they have to choose priorities in aid-giving.

| *Requirements* | *Designers/Suppliers* |
|---|---|
| Around 20 players ideal | Oxfam Education Department |
| Around 1–2 hours | 274 Banbury Road |
| Mimeographed material plus | Oxford |
| 35 mm. slides | OX2 7DZ |

**C Decisions.** A simulation concerning the location of a distribution depot for an oil company.

| *Requirements* | *Designers/Suppliers* |
|---|---|
| 12–24 players | Shell |
| 6–8 hours | Derby House |
| Cased kit | Bletchingley |
| | Surrey |

**B+ Democracy (Legislature).** There are eight variations of the basic game of Democracy. Each variation is self-sufficient or it may be combined to form a series of simulated legislative and community meetings.

| *Requirements* | *Designers/Suppliers* |
|---|---|
| 6 or more players | 4H Foundation |
| 30 minutes (min.) | 7100 Connecticut Avenue NW |
| | Washington DC 20015 |
| | USA |

**B Democracy (Revised Edition).** A simulation of the processes involved in representative government. The game can be played at a number of different levels which either focus on a particular aspect of the democratic process or add elements to the basic legislative model to make a more complex simulation.

| *Requirements* | *Designers/Suppliers* |
|---|---|
| 6–11 players | Western Publishing Co. |
| ½–4 hours | School and Library Department |
| Packaged materials | 850 Third Avenue |
| | New York |
| | NY 10022 |
| | USA |

**B+ Destiny.** A simulation of the historical situation surrounding the American foreign policy reactions to the Cuban Crisis of 1898.

| *Requirements* | *Designers/Suppliers* |
|---|---|
| 20–30 players | Interact |
| 2–8 hours | P O Box 262 |
| Packaged materials | Lakeside |
| | California 92020 |
| | U S A |

**B. Development Game.** A simulation of old-style colonial exploitation in an under-developed area.

| *Requirements* | *Designers/Suppliers* |
|---|---|
| 6–8 players | In *Games in Geography*, |
| 60–80 minutes | Rex Walford (1969), |
| Printed rules and instructions | Longman |

**A+ Dig.** A simulation exercise which calls upon the students to design parts of an archaeological reconstruction relating to a vanished civilization.

| *Requirements* | *Designers/Suppliers* |
|---|---|
| 10–20 players | Interact |
| 2–4 hours | P O Box 262 |
| Packaged materials | Lakeside |
| | California 92020 |
| | U S A |

**B+ Dirty Water.** A decision-making exercise centred on water pollution problems on a city-wide scale.

| *Requirements* | *Designers/Suppliers* |
|---|---|
| 2–4 players | Urban Systems Inc. |
| 1–2 hours | 1033 Massachusetts Avenue |
| Mimeographed materials and playing board | Massachusetts 02138 |
| | U S A |

**B+** **Discovery.** A teaching unit which includes a simulation of early American colonization.

| *Requirements* | *Designers/Suppliers* |
|---|---|
| 30–35 players | Interact |
| 10–15 hours | P O Box 262 |
| Kit of materials | Lakeside |
| | California |
| | USA |

**B+** **Disunia.** A simulation of a possible twenty-first century situation which parallels some of the sovereignty problems which arose in the United States between 1781 and 1789.

| *Requirements* | *Designers/Suppliers* |
|---|---|
| 10–35 players (approx.) | Interact |
| 4–16 hours | P O Box 262 |
| Packaged materials | Lakeside |
| | California 92020 |
| | USA |

**B+** **Division.** A simulation of historical events in the United States at the time of the American Civil War. Procedures concentrate on the divisive political issues of the 1850s and on the crisis election of 1860.

| *Requirements* | *Designers/Suppliers* |
|---|---|
| 10–35 players (approx.) | Interact |
| 4–16 hours | P O Box 262 |
| Packaged materials | Lakeside |
| | California 92020 |
| | USA |

**C+** **Dominoe War Game.** A student war game on the theme of the post-Second World War struggles in Vietnam and Rhodesia.

| *Requirements* | *Designers/Suppliers* |
|---|---|
| 20–60 players | D. S. C. Arthur |
| 4–8 hours | Greenfields High School |
| Mimeographed materials | Cumbernauld |
| | Stirling |
| | Scotland |

**C+ Economic Decision Games.** A series of eight games designed to make the principles of economics more alive with respect to the questions of: the Market, the Firm, Collective Bargaining, the Community, Scarcity and Allocation, Banking, the National Economy and International Trade.

| *Requirements* | *Designers/Suppliers* |
|---|---|
| 6 players and more | Science Research Associates Ltd |
| 2–3 hours | Reading Road |
| Packaged materials | Henley-on-Thames |
| | Oxfordshire |

**B+ Economic System.** This game simulates some of the basic features common to a wide variety of economic systems. Each round in the game consists of three stages – production, marketing and consumption – during which food and manufactured goods are produced, exchanged and consumed.

| *Requirements* | *Designers/Suppliers* |
|---|---|
| 7–13 players | Western Publishing Co. Inc. |
| 2–4 hours | School and Library Department |
| Packaged materials | 850 Third Avenue |
| | New York |
| | NY 10022 |
| | USA |

**B+ Ecopolis.** A teaching unit which includes a simulation of ecological history and of problems in a contemporary environment.

| *Requirements* | *Designers/Suppliers* |
|---|---|
| 30–35 players | Interact |
| 10–15 hours | PO Box 262 |
| Kit of materials | Lakeside |
| | California |
| | USA |

**B+ Election Campaign Game.** A simulation of political activities involved in a presidential election in a fictitious area with fifty electoral constituencies.

| *Requirements* | *Designers/Suppliers* |
| --- | --- |
| 2–20 players | Dr J. P. Cole |
| 1–2 hours | Department of Geography |
| Simple explanatory manual | University of Nottingham |
| | University Park |
| | Nottingham |
| | Also: |
| | In *Ideas in Geography*, |
| | no. 36, pp. 8–12 |

**B Empire.** A game modelled on economic aspects of trade affecting British subjects in the process of becoming American citizens.

| *Requirements* | *Designers/Suppliers* |
| --- | --- |
| 10–50 players | Education Development Centre |
| 2–3 hours | 15 Mifflin Place |
| Mimeographed materials | Cambridge |
| | Massachusetts 02138 |
| | USA |

**B+ Equality.** A simulation of life in the mythical city of Independence, which leads to consideration of the struggle for racial equality in a typical American city. It includes readings, discussions, etc. within the teaching unit.

| *Requirements* | *Designers/Suppliers* |
| --- | --- |
| 30–35 players | Interact |
| 10–15 hours | P O Box 262 |
| Kit of materials | Lakeside |
| | California |
| | USA |

**C Esso Students Business Game.** A business simulation written specifically for students with no business experience in order to give them understanding of:
(a) the interaction of decisions in finance, production, marketing and labour relations;
(b) the team nature of management;
(c) the use of accounting procedures.

| *Requirements* | *Designers/Suppliers* |
|---|---|
| 12–30 players | CRAC |
| 3–5 hours | Bateman Street, |
| | Cambridge |

Packaged materials available
from Esso

**C Export Drive.** A simulation in which participants role-play exporters competing in different world markets, and seeking alternative routes to sell their goods.

| *Requirements* | *Designers/Suppliers* |
|---|---|
| 30–36 players (5 or 6 in each | In *Games in Geography*, |
| group) | Rex Walford (1969), |
| 2–3 hours | Longman |

Printed rules and instructions

**B+ Explorers I.** A simulation of the exploring process in early North America (Explorers II is a similar simulation, based on South American experiences).

| *Requirements* | *Designers/Suppliers* |
|---|---|
| 18–35 players | Project Simile |
| 4–5 hours | PO Box 1023 |
| | |
| Kit of printed materials | La Jolla |
| | California |
| | USA |

**C+ Farming.** A simulation of farm management in Western Kansas at three different time periods. Part of Unit 2 High School Geography Project produced by the Association of American Geographers.

| *Requirements* | *Designers/Suppliers* |
|---|---|
| 15–30 players | The Macmillan Company |
| 40–50 hours | 866 Third Avenue |
| Packaged materials | New York |
| | NY 10022 |
| | USA |
| | Also: |
| | Collier-Macmillan Ltd |
| | Highgate |
| | London |

**B+ Free Enterprise.** A two-phase overlapping simulation which can be used as two separate games. The first, a small retailer, simulates decision making, and the second game assumes the player is simulating a small manufacturer involved in wholesale transactions.

| *Requirements* | *Designers/Suppliers* |
|---|---|
| Mimeographed materials and | BOCES |
| computer facilities | Center for Educational Services |
| | and Research |
| | 845 Fox Meadow Road |
| | Yorktown Heights |
| | NY 10598 |
| | USA |

**C Galapagos (Evolution).** A simulation of the evolution of Darwin's finches in which players fill a scientific role and are required to predict the evolution rate.

| *Requirements* | *Designers/Suppliers* |
|---|---|
| 6–50 players | Abt Associates Inc. |
| 1–2 hours | 14 Concord Lane |
| Mimeographed materials | Cambridge |
| | Massachusetts |
| | USA |

**B+ Generation Gap.** A simulation concentrating on the interaction likely to exist between parents and their adolescent child with respect to issues which commonly reveal opposing generation attitudes.

| *Requirements* | *Designers/Suppliers* |
|---|---|
| 4–10 players | Western Publishing Co. Inc. |
| ½–1 hour | School and Library Department |
| Packaged materials | 850 Third Avenue |
| | New York |
| | N Y 10022 |
| | USA |

**B+ Ghetto.** A city-slum simulation concerned with the dynamics of inner-city community organization. Players allocate their time among activity alternatives to meet basic needs.

| *Requirements* | *Designers/Suppliers* |
|---|---|
| 7–10 players | Western Publishing Co. |
| 2–4 hours | School and Library Department |
| Packaged materials | 850 Third Avenue |
| | New York |
| | N Y 10022 |
| | USA |

**B+ Homesteaders.** A simulation of the life of homesteaders in the Western USA in the 1870s and 1880s.

| *Requirements* | *Designers/Suppliers* |
|---|---|
| 18–35 players | Project Simile |
| 5–7 hours | P O Box 1023 |
| List of printed materials | La Jolla |
| | California |
| | USA |

**B+ Import.** A simulation of the activities of six importing firms located in various parts around the world.

| *Requirements* | *Designers/Suppliers* |
|---|---|
| 18–35 players | Project Simile |
| 6–10 hours | P O Box 1023 |
| Kit of printed materials | La Jolla |
| | California |
| | USA |

**C+ Inner City Planning.** A role-playing simulation of urban renewal processes in the USA involving various community interest groups.

| *Requirements* | *Designers/Suppliers* |
|---|---|
| 12–40 players | The Macmillan Company |
| 1½–3 hours | 866 Third Avenue |
| Published materials | New York |
| | NY 10022 |
| | USA |
| | Also: |
| | Collier-Macmillan Ltd |
| | Highgate |
| | London |

**B+ In Other People's Shoes.** A set of simulated situations which call upon the participants to state, role-play or act out their responses to conflict problems in interpersonal relations.

| *Requirements* | *Designers/Suppliers* |
|---|---|
| 2 players | Moral Education Curriculum Project |
| 30 minutes | University of Oxford |
| Published material | Institute of Education |
| | 15 Norham Gardens |
| | Oxford |
| | (Longman) |

**C+ INS (Inter-Nation Simulation) Kit.** A simulation of the processes of foreign relations and world politics.

| *Requirements* | *Designers/Suppliers* |
|---|---|
| 10–35 players | Science Research Associates Inc. |
| 15–30 hours | Reading Road |
| Packaged kit | Henley-on-Thames |
| | Oxfordshire |

**B Iron and Steel Game.** Students take industrial location decisions at three moments in history.

| *Requirements* | *Designers/Suppliers* |
|---|---|
| 6–8 players in each group. | B. P. Fitzgerald in |
| 45–60 minutes | *Profile* |
| Mimeographed materials | c/o St Mary's and St Paul's |
| | Geographical Society |
| | St Paul's College |
| | Cheltenham |
| | Gloucestershire |

**B+ Life Career Game.** A simulation of aspects of the American labour market, education and marriage opportunities.

| *Requirements* | *Designers/Suppliers* |
|---|---|
| 2–20 players | Western Publishing Co. Inc. |
| 1–6 hours | School and Library Department |
| Packaged materials | 850 Third Avenue |
| | New York |
| | N Y 10022 |
| | USA |

**C+ Location of the Metfab Company.** A simulation designed as an integral part of Unit 2 of the High School Geography Project for the Association of American Geographers. The central feature of the simulation is a hypothetical metal-fabricating company facing the problem of determining a new site for a company branch.

| *Requirements* | *Designers/Suppliers* |
|---|---|
| 5–10 players per group | The Macmillan Company |
| 4–6 hours (40-minute min. | 866 Third Avenue |
| periods) | New York |
| Packaged materials | N Y 10022 |
| | USA |
| | Also: |
| | Collier-Macmillan Ltd |
| | Highgate |
| | London |

**C+ Low Bidder.** A packaged simulation of contract bidding in the construction industry.

| *Requirements* | *Designers/Suppliers* |
|---|---|
| 2–25 players with 3–8 preferable | Entelek Inc. |
| 30 minutes (min.) | 42 Pleasant Street |
| Packaged materials | Newburyport |
| | Massachusetts 01950 |
| | USA |

**C Lugs (Land Use Gaming Simulation).** An anglicized derivative of the basic C L U G model involving the simulation of selected and well defined urban development characteristics.

*Requirements*
4 players (min.)
3 hours (min.)

Printed rules and
operating instructions

*Designers/Suppliers*
Dr J. L. Taylor
Department of Town and Regional
Planning
University of Sheffield
Sheffield
S10 2TN

Also:
In *Instructional Planning Systems*,
J. L. Taylor, Cambridge University
Press, 1971

**B+ Macrotopia.** A world airlines game designed primarily to introduce the complexity of negotiations and transactions between countries to political geographers.

*Requirements*
5–7 players
for the basic game
1–2 hours

Simple mimeographed materials

*Designers/Suppliers*
Dr J. P. Cole
Department of Geography
University of Nottingham
University Park
Nottingham

**B+ Make Your Own World or Man in His Environment.** An eleven-team game presenting environmental conflicts and value choices as part of the Coca-Cola Ecology Kit. The kit was designed in the USA with the aid of the University of Georgia's Institute of Ecology and a British version called 'Man in his Environment' was issued in 1971.

*Requirements*
11 players (min.)
1–2 hours

Kit of materials

*Designers/Suppliers*
Coca-Cola
515 Madison Avenue
New York
N Y
USA

Also:
Coca-Cola Export Corp.
Atlantic House
7 Rockley Road
London
W14 0DH

**C+ Manchester.** A simulation of the impact on the agricultural population of some of the major historical and social issues surrounding the advent of the Industrial Revolution in England.

| *Requirements* | *Designers/Suppliers* |
|---|---|
| 8–40 players | Abt Associates Inc. (for |
| 1–2 hours | Educational Services Inc.) |
| Instructional manual | 14 Concord Lane |
| | Cambridge |
| | Massachusetts |
| | USA |

**C+ Marketplace.** A simulation of the American economic system at work in a medium size, urban manufacturing community.

| *Requirements* | *Designers/Suppliers* |
|---|---|
| 30–50 players | Joint Council on Economic |
| 3–4 hours (min.) | Education |
| Packaged materials | 1212 Avenue of the Americas |
| | New York |
| | NY 10036 |
| | USA |

**B+ Mission.** A simulation of American reactions to issues surrounding United States foreign policy in the Far East and in particular on the current Vietnam situation.

| *Requirements* | *Designers/Suppliers* |
|---|---|
| 10–35 players | Interact |
| 2–4 hours | PO Box 262 |
| Packaged materials | Lakeside |
| | California 92020 |
| | USA |

**B+ Mythia.** A world affairs game which simulates a 'mythical' world yet analogous in many ways to the real world.

| *Requirements* | *Designers/Suppliers* |
|---|---|
| 2–4 hours | American Institutes for Research |
| Mimeographed materials | PO Box 1113 |
| | Palo Alto |
| | California 94302 |
| | USA |

**C+ National Economy Game.** A simulation game representing the functioning of the British national economy in terms of land, labour and capital.

| *Requirements* | *Designers/Suppliers* |
|---|---|
| 10 players (min.) | Dr Ian Bracken |
| 1 hour (min.) | Department of Town Planning |
| Do-it-yourself materials | Institute of Science and Technology |
| | University of Wales |
| | Cardiff |

**C+ National Management Game.** An inter-school management game for groups of various ages concentrating on the corporate nature of planning and control. The school version is based on the ICL BME–1 package and is jointly sponsored by the *Financial Times*, the Institute of Chartered Accountants in England and Wales and International Computers Limited.

| *Requirements* | *Designers/Suppliers* |
|---|---|
| Very flexible numbers | International Computers Ltd |
| 4–5 hours (min.) | Bridge House |
| Packaged materials | Putney Bridge |
| | London |
| | SW15 |
| | Information from the Institute of |
| | Chartered Accountants |

**B+ Neighborhood.** A simulation of aspects of urban development at the local level involving problems of physical planning and social organization.

| *Requirements* | *Designers/Suppliers* |
|---|---|
| 4–12 players | Wellesley School Curriculum Center |
| 1–2 hours | 12 Seaward Road |
| Mimeographed materials | Wellesley Hills |
| | Massachusetts 02181 |
| | USA |
| | Also: |
| | Abt Associates Inc. |
| | 14 Concord Lane |
| | Cambridge |
| | Massachusetts |
| | USA |

**B** **North Sea Gas.** A game using the gas explorations of the North Sea as a context for a simulation about basic problems of mineral exploitation.

| *Requirements* | *Designers/Suppliers* |
|---|---|
| 30–36 players (5 or 6 groups) | In *Games in Geography*, |
| 60–80 minutes | Rex Walford (1969), |
| Printed rules and instructions | Longman |

**C** **Panatina.** A simulation of an imaginary South American nation in which players face such problems as land reform, revolution and a Common Market proposal.

| *Requirements* | *Designers/Suppliers* |
|---|---|
| 18–35 players | Project Simile |
| 5–6 hours | PO Box 1023 |
| Kit of printed materials | La Jolla |
| | California |
| | USA |

**B+** **Panic.** A simulation covering major aspects of American social, economic and political history in the period between 1920 and 1940. Procedures concentrate on the prospects of the 1920s contrasted with the depression of the 1930s.

| *Requirements* | *Designers/Suppliers* |
|---|---|
| 10–35 players | Interact |
| 3–10 hours | PO Box 262 |
| Packaged materials | Lakeside |
| | California 92020 |
| | USA |

**B+** **Plans.** An influence allocation game simulating the interaction between Military, Civil Rights, National, International, Business and Labour interests in American Society.

| *Requirements* | *Designers/Suppliers* |
|---|---|
| 12–30 players | Project Simile PO Box 1023 |
| 3–8 hours | 1150 Silverado |
| An instructional manual plus pro forma | La Jolla |
| | California 92037 |
| | USA |

**C+ Point Roberts.** A simulation of international boundary arbitration procedures produced as part of Unit 4 of the High School Geography Project organized by the Association of American Geographers.

*Requirements*
30 players
30–50 hours
Packaged materials

*Designers/Suppliers*
The Macmillan Company
866 Third Avenue
New York
N Y 10022
USA

Also:
Collier-Macmillan Ltd
Highgate
London

**B+ Pollution.** A simulation covering some of the major social, political, and economic problems involved in attempts to control pollution.

*Requirements*
12–24 players
2–4 hours
Mimeographed materials

*Designers/Suppliers*
Wellesley School Curriculum Center
12 Seaward Road
Wellesley Hills
Massachusetts 02181
USA

Also:
Abt Associates Inc.
14 Concord Lane
Cambridge
Massachusetts
USA

**C+ Politica.** A political crisis simulation set in Latin America and involving major inter-nation conflicts.

*Requirements*
40–80 players
2–4 hours
Mimeographed materials

*Designers/Suppliers*
Abt Associates Inc.
14 Concord Lane
Cambridge
Massachusetts
USA

**C+** **Portsville.** An interactive game produced by the Association of American Geographers as part of Unit 1 of the High School Geography Project and designed to simulate the growth of the City of PORTSVILLE in three different time periods.

*Requirements*
6 players per map board
8–10 hours (40min. minimum periods)
Packaged materials

*Designers/Suppliers*
The Macmillan Company
866 Third Avenue
New York
NY 10022
USA

Also:
Collier-Macmillan Ltd
Highgate
London

**B+** **Population.** A board game designed to simulate some of the problems of overpopulation likely to occur in a rapidly developing country.

*Requirements*
4 players (min.)
1–2 hours
Packaged materials

*Designers/Suppliers*
Urban Systems Inc.
1033 Massachusetts Avenue
Cambridge
Massachusetts 02138
USA

**B+** **Powderhorn.** An adaptation of the well-known Starpower simulation. Students take the part of frontiersmen who establish a three-tiered society by trading rifles, traps and pelts.

*Requirements*
18–35 players
1 hour plus
Kit of printed materials

*Designers/Suppliers*
Project Simile
PO Box 1023
La Jolla
California
USA

**B  Railway Pioneers.** A simulation using the North American railway building of the 1860s as a context for consideration of problems of route building.

| *Requirements* | *Designers/Suppliers* |
| --- | --- |
| 30–35 players | Longman Group Ltd |
| (5–6 in each group) | Longman House |
| 60–80 minutes | Burnt Mill |
| Packaged materials, printed rules and instructions in teachers' manual | Harlow |
| | Essex |
| | Also: |
| | In *Games in Geography*, |
| | Rex Walford (1969), |
| | Longman |

**B+  Regular Diffusion.** Simulation procedures which present a mechanical view of the spread of a new idea (innovation) about a prescribed area.

| *Requirements* | *Designers/Suppliers* |
| --- | --- |
| 1–2 players | Dr J. P. Cole |
| ½–1 hour | Department of Geography |
| Simple explanatory notes | Nottingham University |
| | University Park |
| | Nottingham |

**B+  Roaring Camp.** A simulation of life in a nineteenth-century mining community in western USA.

| *Requirements* | *Designers/Suppliers* |
| --- | --- |
| 18–35 players | Project Simile |
| 5–6 hours | PO Box 1023 |
| Kit of printed materials | La Jolla |
| | California |
| | USA |

**C+ Rutile and the Beach.** A simulation of Australian mining, conservation and recreation groups in competition for land. Part of Unit 5 of the High School Geography Project, produced by the Association of American Geographers.

| *Requirements* | *Designers/Suppliers* |
|---|---|
| 27 player roles | The Macmillan Company |
| 50–60 hours (40 min. minimum periods) | 866 Third Avenue |
| | New York |
| Packaged materials | N Y 10022 |
| | USA |
| | Also: |
| | Collier-Macmillan Ltd |
| | Highgate |
| | London |

**C+ Section.** A simulation designed to provide students with an understanding of conflicts of interest among the sections of a political territory as they are expressed in the political process Used in Unit 4 of the American High School Geography Project produced by the Association of American Geographers.

| *Requirements* | *Designers/Suppliers* |
|---|---|
| Over 30 players | The Macmillan Company |
| 5–6 hours | 866 Third Avenue |
| | New York |
| Packaged materials | N Y 10022 |
| | USA |
| | Also: |
| | Collier-Macmillan Ltd |
| | Highgate |
| | London |

**A+ Shopping.** A game using the local shopping centre to consider problems of central business districts and route efficiency.

| *Requirements* | *Designers/Suppliers* |
|---|---|
| Individual players | In *Games in Geography*, |
| 20–30 minutes | Rex Walford (1969) |
| Printed rules and instructions | Longman |

**B Sierra Leone.** A simulation which places the student in a succession of decision-making roles in modern Sierra Leone. As decision-making proficiency is demonstrated so the student proceeds to more advanced tasks related to the management of a less developed economy.

| *Requirements* | *Designers/Suppliers* |
|---|---|
| 1 player | BOCES |
| 5–8 hours | Center for Educational Services and Research |
| Multi-media materials and computer facilities | 845 Fox Meadow Road |
| | Yorktown Heights |
| | New York 10598 |
| | USA |

**C+ Simulation of American Government.** A simulation of certain hypothetical roles and relationships analogous to those found in various branches of American government.

| *Requirements* | *Designers/Suppliers* |
|---|---|
| 9 players and above | Dale M. Garvey |
| 2–4 hours | Division of Social Sciences |
| Mimeographed materials | Kansas State Teachers College |
| | Emporia |
| | Kansas |
| | USA |

**B+ Sitte.** An influence allocation game simulating the impact of five interest groups on the changing quality of life in the mythical city of Sitte.

| *Requirements* | *Designers/Suppliers* |
|---|---|
| 17+ players | Project Simile PO Box 1023 |
| 2–4 hours | 1150 Silverado |
| Packaged materials | La Jolla |
| | California 92037 |
| | USA |

**B Smog.** An elementary simulation of atmospheric pollution problems encountered by city administrators.

| *Requirements* | *Designers/Suppliers* |
|---|---|
| 2–4 players | Urban Systems Inc. |
| 1–2 hours | 1033 Massachusetts Avenue |
| Mimeographed materials and playing board | Cambridge |
| | Massachusetts 02138 |
| | USA |

C+ **Solution for Acme Metal.** A simulation of flood prevention planning designed as an integral part of Unit 5 of the High School Geography Project, produced by the Association of American Geographers.

| *Requirements* | *Designers/Suppliers* |
|---|---|
| 7–28 players | The Macmillan Company |
| 30–40 hours (40 minute | 866 Third Avenue |
| minimum periods) | New York |
| | N Y 10022 |
| Packaged materials | U S A |
| | Also: |
| | Collier-Macmillan Ltd |
| | Highgate |
| | London |

B **Spring Green Motorway.** A role-playing game simulating reactions to the route of a proposed motorway through the village of Spring Green.

| *Requirements* | *Designers/Suppliers* |
|---|---|
| 24 players | Community Service Volunteers |
| 2–3 hours | 28 Commercial Street |
| | London |
| Packaged materials | E1 |

B **Starpower.** A societal advancement game which simulates community mobility and power structures.

| *Requirements* | *Designers/Suppliers* |
|---|---|
| 18–35 players | Project Simile P O Box 1023 |
| 2–4 hours | 1150 Silverado |
| | La Jolla |
| Packaged materials | California 92037 |
| | U S A |

C **Steam.** A simulation of some of the economic aspects of steam-engine development relevant to coal mining in England at the commencement of the nineteenth century.

| *Requirements* | *Designers/Suppliers* |
|---|---|
| 6–15 players | Abt Associates Inc. |
| 1–2 hours | 14 Concord Lane |
| | Cambridge |
| Mimeographed materials | Massachusetts |
| | U S A |

**B+ Streets Ahead.** A simulation of city problems which can be played at two levels:
*Short Cut*, a straight-forward table game lasting approximately an hour; or,
*Long Way Round*, an exercise that could last a term or even a year.

| *Requirements* | *Designers/Suppliers* |
|---|---|
| 6 players or groups | Dr E. C. Midwinter |
| 1 hour | Liverpool Educational Priority |
| Packaged materials | Area Project |
| | Paddington Comprehensive |
| | School |
| | Liverpool |
| | L7 3EA |

**B Sumerian Game.** This simulation requires the student to take the role of town ruler about 3500 BC. In this role the student is faced with a variety of elementary community development problems.

| *Requirements* | *Designers/Suppliers* |
|---|---|
| 1 player | BOCES |
| 5–8 hours | Center for Educational Services |
| Computer and multi-media | and Research |
| facilities required. | 845 Fox Meadow Road |
| | Yorktown Heights |
| | NY 10598 |
| | USA |

**B+ Sunshine.** A simulation in which each participant is 'born' into the community of a town called Sunshine. Different racial and community identities are assumed and the game revolves around various community development problems and their impact on roles and relationships.

| *Requirements* | *Designers/Suppliers* |
|---|---|
| 10–35 players | Interact |
| 9–16 hours | PO Box 262 |
| Packaged materials | Lakeside |
| | California 92020 |
| | USA |

**B+ Mr Trustworthy's Farm.** A simple game in which pupils simulate the problems of an English farmer.

| *Requirements* | *Designers/Suppliers* |
| --- | --- |
| Individual players | P. J. Wagland in *Profile* |
| 45 mins–60 mins | c/o St Mary's and St Paul's |
| Mimeographed materials | Geographical Society |
| | St Paul's College, |
| | Cheltenham |
| | Gloucestershire |

**C+ Venture.** A school business game which is a total enterprise simulation covering many of the major decision-making areas of business and management.

| *Requirements* | *Designers/Suppliers* |
| --- | --- |
| 20–35 players | Public Relations Depart. |
| 4–5 hours | (Education Services) |
| Complete kit available without charge in the USA | The Procter & Gamble Co. |
| | PO Box 599 |
| | Cincinnati |
| | Ohio 45201 |
| | USA |

**B+ World Democracy.** A multi-nation crisis game of international relations with scenarios for each of the six participating countries.

| *Requirements* | *Designers/Suppliers* |
| --- | --- |
| 6–36 players | P. J. Tansey |
| 2–4 hours | Berkshire College of Education |
| Mimeographed operational instructions. | Reading |
| | Also: |
| | Society for Academic Gaming & Simulation in Education and Training |
| | c/o 5 Errington |
| | Moreton-in-Marsh |
| | Gloucestershire |

**C  Yes, But Not Here.** A role-playing simulation of an urban locational conflict involving a housing project for the elderly.

| *Requirements* | *Designers/Suppliers* |
| --- | --- |
| 32 roles | The Macmillan Company |
| 2–3 hours | 866 Third Avenue |
| Published materials | New York |
| | N Y 10022 |
| | U S A |
| | Also: |
| | Collier-Macmillan Ltd |
| | Highgate |
| | London |

# Bibliographies

P. J. Tansey and D. Unwin (eds.), 'Bibliography of simulation and gaming in education', *British Journal of Education Studies* June 1969.

P. J. Tansey and D. Unwin (eds.), *Simulation and Gaming in Education, Training and Business: A Bibliography*, New University of Ulster, 1969.

J. L. Taylor (ed.), *Social Science Instructional Simulation Systems: A Selected Bibliography*, S U R I S S project, University of Sheffield, 1969.

P. Twelker (ed.), *Instructional Simulation Systems: An Annotated Bibliography*, Continuing Education Publications, Corvallis, Oregon.

D. Unwin, 'Simulations and games: descriptions and sources', in P. J. Tansey (ed.), *Educational Aspects of Simulation*, McGraw-Hill, 1971.

R. Werner and J. J. Werner (eds.), *Bibliography of Simulations: Social Systems and Education*, Western Behavioral Sciences Institute, La Jolla, California, 1969.

J. P. Wilson, D. E. Adams and F. L. Norton, *A Selected Bibliography of Simulations and Related Subjects (1960–69)*, Political Science Department, Kansas State College, Pittsburg, Kansas 66702. Also Appendix, 1971.

R. Zieler (ed.), *Games for School Use* (revised by Irene Strum), B O C E S, 845 Fox Meadow Road, Yorktown Heights, New York 10598.

D. W. Zuckerman and R. E. Horn (eds.) *The Guide to Simulation Games for Education and Training*, Information Resources Inc., Cambridge, Massachusetts 02138, 1970. United Kingdom and European Distributors: Richard S. Gothard and Company Ltd, Gothard House, Henley-on-Thames, Oxford, RG9 1AJ.

# Film and Video-Tape Material
## (available from British Sources)

Several video-tapes of simulation material are held in the libraries of colleges of education and polytechnics. They may often be unavailable for a variety of reasons, but it may be possible to arrange to view such material by a prior negotiation with the commissioning tutor of the video-tape, and/or with the A V A department of the college/polytechnic concerned.

### '... And Gladly Teach'

E V R cassettes of eight programmes of a Harlech T V series for teachers which used simulation. Each cassette contains two programmes. Available for purchase from E V R Partnership, Vogue House, 1 Hanover Square, London, 1 R0JH and from Rank Bush Murphy Ltd, Power Road, Chiswick, London, W4. Available on loan from Guild Sound and Vision, Kingston Rd, London, SW19, 3NR.

### The Business Game

16 mm film of the forerunner of the National Management Game, lasting for 25 minutes. Covers schools competing in the game. Loan copies available from The Administrator, The National Management Game, I C L Bridge House South, Putney Bridge, London, SW6.

### Horizon: A Game of War

16 mm film, lasting for 60 minutes. Covers a simulation of the contemporary Arab-Israeli conflict. Available for purchase from B B C Television Enterprises, Villiers House, Haven Green, London, W5.

### New Insights

35 mm film, lasting 25 minutes. Covers pupils using a variety of approaches including simulations, with material from the American High School Geography Project. Available on loan from Collier-Macmillan Ltd, Highgate, London.

# Series Publications

*Cambridge Monographs* A series sponsored and produced by the Cambridge Institute of Education. Occasional volumes have been devoted to simulation and gaming, i.e.

Armstrong, R. H. R., and Taylor, J. L. (1970), *Instructional Simulation Systems in Higher Education*, Cambridge Monographs on Teaching Methods, 2.

Armstrong, R. H. R., and Taylor, J. L. (1971), *Feedback on Instructional Simulation Systems*, Cambridge Monographs on Teaching Methods, 5.

*National Gaming Council Proceedings* An annual publication organized by the American based National Gaming Council and sponsored by a different agency each year.

*Occasional Newsletter about Simulation and Games* (formerly the *Occasional Newsletter about Uses of Simulations and Games for Education and Training*) Edited and produced by Western Behavioral Sciences Institute, La Jolla, California. An informal and yet world-wide channel of communication which commenced publication in 1965 and still continues to be a valuable source of information.

*S A G S E T Newsletter* An occasional publication of the British-based Society for Academic Gaming and Simulation in Education and Training.

*Simulation and Games* Published by Sage Publications, Beverly Hills, California. An international journal of theory, design and research which commenced publication in 1970 and shows every sign of becoming the one authoritative journal in the field.

*Simulation Gaming News* Published five times a year, an informal tabloid, newspaper-format publication. Box 8899, Stanford, California 94305.

*Simulation in the Service of Society* Managing Editor: John McLeod; Editors: Roland and Joan Werner. Box 994, La Jolla, California 92037. A new monthly newsletter which commenced publication in January 1971.

# References and Further Reading

This list of references does not include references to articles which are *only* the description of a game. For these, see Part Three.

ABT, C. (1966), 'Games for learning: Social Studies Curriculum Project', Occasional paper no. 7, Educational Services Inc., Cambridge, Massachusetts.

ABT, C. (1968), *Final Report on The Virgin Islands Game*, Abt Associates, Cambridge, Massachusetts.

ABT, C. (1970), *Serious Games*, Viking Press.

ARMSTRONG, R. H. R., and TAYLOR, J. L. (eds. (1970), *Instructional Simulation Systems in Higher Education*, Cambridge Monographs on Education, no. 2.

ARMSTRONG, R. H. R., and TAYLOR, J. L. (eds.) (1971), *Feedback on Instructional Simulation Systems*, Cambridge Monographs on Education, no. 5.

AVEDON, E. M., and SUTTON-SMITH, B. (1971), *The Study of Games*, Wiley.

American High School Geography Project (1971), *Geography in an Urban Age*, Units 1–6, Macmillan.

BARNES, D., BRITTON, J., ROSEN, H., and the LATE (1969), *Language, the Learner and the School*, Penguin.

BERNE, E. (1968), *Games People Play*, Deutsch; Penguin, 1968.

BOOCOCK, S., and SCHILD, E. O. (eds.) (1968), *Simulation Games in Learning*, Sage.

BRUNER, J. S. (1960), *The Process of Education*, Vintage Books.

BRUNER, J. S. (1967), *Towards a Theory of Instruction*, Norton.

CAILLOIS, R. (1961), *Man, Play and Games*, Free Press.

CARLSON, E. (1969), *Learning Through Games*, Public Affairs Press, Washington D.C.

CHERRYHOLMES, C. H. (1966), 'Some current research on the effectiveness of educational simulations', *American Behavioral Scientist*, vol. 10, no. 2, pp. 4–7.

COLE J. P., and BEYNON, N. J. (1969–72), *New Ways in Geography*, Introductory Book, Books I, II, III and Teachers' Book, Blackwell.

COLEMAN, J. (1968), *Simulation Games and Social Theory* (Report no. 8) and *Games as Vehicles for Social Theory* (Report no. 21), Johns Hopkins University, Center for the Study of Social Organization of Schools.

COPELAND M (1969), *The Game of Nations*, Weidenfeld & Nicolson.

CRUICKSHANK, D. B. (1966), 'Simulation, new direction in teacher preparation', *Phi Delta Kappan*, vol. 48, pp. 23–4.

DALTON, R. et al. (1972), *Simulation Games in Geography*, Macmillan.

DEMBITZER, B. (1971), 'The Guyana trade game', in R. H. R. Armstrong and J. L. Taylor (eds.), *Feedback on Instructional Simulation Systems*, Cambridge Monographs on Education, no. 5.

FEATHERSTONE, D. F. (1962), *War Games*, Stanley Paul.

FINES, J. (1970), 'American development projects in the social studies', *Journal of Curriculum Studies*, vol. 2, no. 1.

GORDON, A. K. (1968), *Educational Games Extension Service*, Units 1–8, S R A, Chicago.

GOULD, P. R. (1963), 'Man and his environment; a game theoretic framework', *Annals of the Association of American Geographers*, September, pp. 290–97. Reprinted in P. J. Ambrose (ed.), *Analytical Human Geography*, Longman, 1969.

GRANT, C. (1971), *The War Game*, Black.

GUETZKOW, H., et al. (1963), *Simulation in International Relations*, Prentice-Hall.

GUNN, A. M. (1971), 'The American High School Geography Project', *Journal of Curriculum Studies*, vol. 3, no. 1.

HELMER, O. (1965), *Social Technology*, Rand Corporation, document no. P–3063, Santa Monica, California; Basic Books, 1967.

HEMPHILL, J. K., GRIFFITHS, D. E., and FREDERIKSEN, N. (1962), *Administrative Performance and Personality: A Study of the Principal in a Simulated Elementary School*, Teachers' College, Columbia University.

HERRON, R., and SUTTON-SMITH, B. (1971), *Child's Play*, Wiley.

HUIZINGA, J. (1944), *Homo Ludens*, Paladin.

KASPERSON, R. E. (1968), 'Games as educational media', *Journal of Geography*, vol. 67, no. 7, pp. 409–22.

KAYE, B. (1970), *Participation in Learning*, Allen & Unwin.

KEEBLE, D. (1969), 'School teaching and urban geography; some new approaches', *Geography*, vol. 54, pt 1, pp. 18–33.

KERSH, B. Y. (1962), 'Simulation in teacher education', paper read at the American Psychological Association (mimeo).

KIDDER, S. J. (1971), *Emotional Arousal and Attitude Change During Simulation Games*, Report 3 from the Center for Social Organization for Schools, Johns Hopkins University.

KLEIN, J. (1964), *Working with Groups*, Hutchinson.

LANGLEY, C. (ed.) (1972), *Games and Simulations*, BBC.

McEACHERN, A. W., and TAYLOR, E. M. (1967), *Simbad: A Proposal for Probation*, University of Southern California Youth Studies Centre, Los Angeles.

McLELLAN, J. (1970), *The Question of Play*, Pergamon.

MASON, E. (1970), *Collaborative Learning*, Ward Lock.

MORENO, J. (1947), *The Theatre of Spontaneity* (trs. from *Das Stagrufttheater*), Beacon House.

NICHOLSON, M. (1970), *Conflict Analysis*, Edinburgh University Press.

OPIE, I., and OPIE, P. (1959), *The Lore and Language of School children*, Oxford University Press.

PIAGET, J. (1950), *The Origins of Intelligence in the Child*, Routledge & Kegan Paul.

PIAGET, J. (1951), *Play, Dreams and Imitation in Childhood*, Heinemann.

PESTON, M. E. and CODDINGTON, A. (1967), 'The elementary ideas of game theory', CAS Occasional Paper, no. 6, HMSO.

POOL, I. de S. (1964), 'Simulating social systems', *International Science and Technology*, vol. 27, pp. 62–71.

RASER, J. R. (1969), *Simulation and Society*, Allyn & Bacon.

RICCARDI, F. M., *et al.* (1967), *Top Management Decision Simulation: The AMA Approach*, American Management Association, New York.

SCARFE, N. V. (1971), 'Games, models and reality in the teaching of geography', *Geography*, vol. 56, pp. 191–205.

SCHILD, G. (1971), *The Influence of Games on School Achievement Abilities and Attitudes*, Report 92 from the Center for Social Organization for Schools, Johns Hopkins University.

SHIRTS, G. (1970), 'Games people play', *Saturday Review*, 16 May 1970.

SHUBIK, M. (ed.) (1964), *Game Theory and Related Approaches to Social Behaviour*, Wiley.

SMITH, G., and COLE, J. P. (1967), 'Geographical games', *Bulletin of Quantitative Data for Geographers*, no. 7, Department of Geography, University of Nottingham.

STORM, M. (1971), 'Schools and the community: an issue-based approach', *Bulletin for Environmental Education*, no. 1, Town and Country Planning Association, Education Unit.

TAYLOR, J. L. (1971), *Instructional Planning Systems: A Gaming Simulation Approach to Urban Problems*, Cambridge University Press.

TAYLOR, J. L., and CARTER, K. R. (1971), 'Gaming simulation', *Journal of the Town Planning Institute*, vol. 57, no. 1, pp. 25–34

TAYLOR, L. C. (1971), *Resources for Learning*, Penguin.

TAYLOR, W. (ed.) (1970), *Heading for Change: A Harlech TV Series*, Harlech, Bristol.

TANSEY, P. J. (ed.) (1971), *Educational Aspects of Simulation*, McGraw-Hill.

TANSEY, P. J., and UNWIN, D. (1969), *Simulation and Gaming in Education*, Methuen.

TURNSTILL, J. (1969), *Discovering Wargames*, Shire Publications.

TWELKER, P. A. (1967), 'Classroom simulation and teacher preparation', *School Review*, vol. 75, pp. 197–204.

VYGOTSKY, L. S. (1962), *Thought and Language*, Wiley.

WALFORD, R. A. (1968), 'Decision making', *Geography Teacher (India)*, vol. 4, no. 1, pp. 17–26.

WALFORD, R. A. (1969), *Games in Geography*, Longman.

WALFORD, R. A. (1972), 'Games and simulations', in *New Movements in the Study and Teaching of Geography*, Temple-Smith.

WARD, C., and FYSON, A. (eds.) (1972), *Bulletin of Environment Education*.

WAY, B. (1967), *Development Through Drama*, Longman.

WILSON, A. (1968), *War Gaming* (formerly *The Bomb and the Computer*), Barrie & Rockcliff; Penguin, 1969.

ZUCKERMAN, D., and HORN, R. (1970), 'What is it you want to know?' *Media and Methods*, October. See also Zuckerman and Horn in Bibliography.

Two issues of the *American Behavioral Scientist* have been devoted to Simulation Articles:

October–November 1966, edited by James Coleman, was focused on 'Simulation Games and Learning Behavior';

July–August 1969, edited by M. Irbar and C. Stoll, was focused on 'Social Simulations.'

# Index

# Index